Fragile Elite

Anthropology of Policy

Cris Shore and Susan Wright, editors

Fragile Elite

The Dilemmas of China's Top University Students

Susanne Bregnbæk

Stanford University Press

Stanford, California

Stanford University Press

Stanford, California

Printed in the United States of America on acid-free, archival-quality paper

Library of Congress Cataloging-in-Publication Data

Bregnbaek, Susanne, author.

Fragile elite : the dilemmas of China's top university students / Susanne Bregnbaek.

pages cm.—(Anthropology of policy)

Includes bibliographical references and index.

ISBN 978-0-8047-9607-1 (cloth : alk. paper)—ISBN 978-0-8047-9778-8 (pbk. : alk. paper)

1. College students—China—Beijing—Social conditions. 2. College students—Family relationships—China—Beijing. 3. Education, Higher—Social aspects—China—Beijing. 4. Beijing da xue—Students. 5. Qing hua da xue (Beijing, China)—Students. I. Title.

LA1133.7.B74 2016

378.51′56—dc23

2015017617

ISBN 978-0-8047-9779-5 (electronic)

Typeset by Bruce Lundquist in 10.25/15 Brill

For Benjamin and Peter

Contents

Acknowledgments

THIS BOOK IS THE RESULT of many conversations with friends, family, and colleagues. I am particularly indebted to my Chinese interlocutors, who shared their lives with me and whom I can thank only anonymously. I also warmly wish to thank Hanne Cecilie Berthelsen-Kruse, Edel Bregnbæk, Mogens Bregnbæk, Pernille Brix, Tine Gammeltoft, Teresa Kuan, Claus A. Lassen, Francine Lorimer, Cecilia Milwertz, Lars Møllenbak-Bregnbæk, Nanna Mullamilla, Sissel Lea Nielsen, Michael Puett, Saren, Charles Stafford, Marie Høgh Thøgersen, Ulla Vanges-Schmitt, Ulrika Villaró, and Susan Whyte for different kinds of important support. For tremendous enthusiasm about my book project, I thank Pablo Selaya Elio with love. For feedback on draft versions, I thank my friends and colleagues Ann Benwell, Mikkel Bunkenborg, Morten Hulvej, Nanna Jordt Jørgensen, Anja Kublitz, Hans Lucht, Bjarke Oxlund, Lotte Buch Segal, Kasper Tang-Vangkilde, Stig Thøgersen, Henrik Vigh, and Louise Vogel-Kielgast. I am grateful to the Stanford University Press editors, Sue Wright, Cris Shore, and Michelle Lipinski, for taking an interest in my work. I owe a special debt of gratitude to Michael Jackson for intellectual guidance, support, and friendship. Finally, I thank the Danish Research Council for the Humanities (FKK) and the Asian Dynamics Initiative (ADI) for funding my research.

Fragile Elite

Introduction

A FEW MONTHS INTO MY FIELDWORK IN CHINA,[1] a student at Beijing University committed suicide by jumping from the roof of a tall university building. Almost every young Chinese person dreams of gaining a place at Beijing University or Tsinghua University. These are China's highest-ranked universities, and are regarded as being in a league of their own. Yet student suicide rates at these universities are rumored to be higher than those at other universities.[2]

Beijing University reported the suicide as an "accident." Yet, despite the official silence, students talked about the incident and speculated about the causes. Some people blamed the cutthroat competitiveness of the educational system for the frequent incidents of suicide. Others saw the suicide of elite students as highlighting the flaws of the pampered generation of little emperors and empresses who have been spoiled within the family and are now unable to cope with the vicissitudes of real life. "How could she do this to her parents?" many people wondered. According to one rumor, this girl had left a suicide note for her parents apologizing that she could not live up to their expectations. One story had it that she was about to graduate, but was being bypassed in job interviews because she lacked the kinds of connections that could open doors. Others felt that the real reason behind the suicide had to be a family conflict or a broken love affair. Some students quietly remarked that suicide was really the only way to escape from the pressure.

The suicide and the students' responses to it indicate what is at stake for university students in Beijing and point to critical issues of intergenerational continuity and discontinuity in a nation undergoing radical transformation.

During the last twenty years China has changed from being a poor agricultural country to being a country with the world's second-largest economy. When Deng Xiaoping initiated the period of "Reform and Opening Up," it was assumed that massive investments in higher education and the creation of a qualified elite would guarantee China a place in the first world (Fong 2004). My ethnography explores the implications of the new globally competitive "knowledge economy"—a term coined by the Organisation for Economic Co-operation and Development (OECD) to designate the divide between "hands" (populations doing dirty and dangerous manual labor) and "heads" (populations specializing in knowledge and research). With China's rise to power, this division was destabilized, and the Chinese government now strives to make China prosper not only as the factory of the world but also as an "innovative society." The everyday lives of Chinese have changed utterly, especially in urban areas, and so too have the kinds of lives people aspire to lead, as well as what defines a life worth living.

These societal transformations have also profoundly changed the urban landscape. I vividly remember riding my bicycle to school when I was living in Beijing as a child during the mid-1980s. Having left the walled and gated diplomatic compound, I joined the mass of people dressed mostly in blue or gray Mao-style attire who crowded the wide bicycle lanes, following the slow pace of life. In the winter, engulfed in the chiming of bicycle bells, I would carefully zigzag my way between frozen gobs of spit. I passed a gray *hutong* (traditional courtyard) area and then followed a straight tree-lined road, under a canopy of naked branches. Sometimes my way was blocked by horse carriages, truckloads of vegetables, or bicycle vendors selling baked potatoes or tiny sugar-coated apples on long sticks. Chubby toddlers dressed in thick, colorful fabrics stuck out in the grayness of the urban scenery. Parents would often poke their children to make them notice the foreign child passing by, and students would sometimes follow me in their eagerness to practice a few English phrases. I would pass a small park in which groups of old men carrying birdcages gathered to exercise their birds, and occasionally little old women with small bound feet would pass by, each walking cautiously and supported by a cane.

During my fieldwork in Beijing in 2005 and 2007, I sometimes walked this same stretch, and I was always struck by the uncanny experience of familiarity and strangeness. The familiar road lined with trees was still there. Advertisements and kitsch caught my eye, along with the busy vendors insistently trying to attract customers. Chinese as well as foreign people drank coffee and cocktails at the sidewalk cafés, and beggars (people from the countryside or elderly people in dilapidated Mao suits) roamed the street. Their ghostly presence seemed to be an indication that time was out of joint. Taxis and cars noisily made their way forward as shoppers jumped in and out of them, heading in different directions. A multi-story shopping mall, Pacific Century Place, over-looked the space of the old park, in which public exercise machines had been placed in the shade of the trees.

In 2012, when I last returned for fieldwork, yet another transformation had taken place as the trendy shopping mall and restaurant area called the Village had replaced the old *hutong* area, making even the 1990s bars on the other side of the street look somewhat outdated. Walking in this area, as I passed the shops of famous international brands and restaurants from all over the world, I often felt that I was in a polished world of bling-bling consumption, populated mostly by people who looked as if they had jumped out of the music videos that are shown on huge TV screens. The scenario seemed so utterly removed from the Beijing I used to know. And yet the familiar street was still there and I some-times looked up at the same greenness of the willows while drinking coffee or jotting down notes at a café nearby.

The colorfully dressed toddlers that I remember from my own childhood in Beijing are now young people in their twenties. They belong to what is popularly termed the post-eighties generation (*ba ling hou*) and have been brought up in accordance with the one-child policy and its related educational ideals. These policies have aimed to create a generation[3] of well-educated young people who can pave the way for China's transition to a knowledge economy. What young people in China today share is a common destiny of being predominantly "only" children who have grown up with a promise of social mobility but at the same time face seemingly endless competition vis-à-vis their peers.

In Beijing people from apparently all strata of society, and young people in particular, speak of the pressure (*yali*) of their everyday lives, articulated as a necessity to forge onward in order not to be left behind. I was talking about this problem with Wu Jiao, a student of electrical engineering, as we sat beside the window at a café located on the second floor of a high-rise building with a view of Beijing's elevated train. We watched as crowds of people energetically made their way forward, and he remarked, "We are on a train that is going fast, leaving the past, speeding towards the future, but nobody seems to stop and reflect on where the train is going."

Oedipus in China

My focus in this book is on the "oedipal project" (Brown 1959; Fortes 1981; Jackson 2006:217). This can be understood as the universal existential need to establish some degree of separation from the will of parents and, by extension, the will of the state. In Confucianism the metaphor of the state or nation as a family is crucial. Confucius believed that the child should be subordinate to the parent, the younger brother to the older brother, the wife to the husband, and the subject to the sovereign, who is regarded as the father of the nation. With the leadership of Hu Jintao and Wen Jiabao since 2002 a form of state Confucianism has been reinvented as a way to justify a need for hierarchies and obedience under the rubric of a "harmonious society." While this shift in policy or re-invocation of an older cultural model should be taken into account, I argue that the relationship between state and family has wider implications. Kinship terminology and the connections between the *domus*[4] and the *polis* are crucial to how we imagine relationships with the powers that be. While cultural anthropology conventionally emphasizes cultural particularities, I argue that it is important for anthropology to also address universal phenomena. As Ghassan Hage has noted, the family evokes images of both maternal care and patriarchal control, an ambiguity that is carried over into images of the state (Hage 1996a:472–477). In other words, I expand the oedipal theme to encompass both the parent/child bond and the more explicitly political relationship to the Chinese state, which is in fact often imagined and portrayed as a parental figure exercising care and control (*guan*).

During the first period of fieldwork in 2005, my family and I stayed in a newly built and partly empty twenty-six-story apartment building in the Haidian District in northwest Beijing, which was right next to a primary school. Every morning we would wake up at seven o'clock to the sound of loud classical music coming from the school compound, where the students had gathered for their morning exercise. On Fridays the session was completed with a ceremonial raising of the Chinese flag and the playing of the national anthem. This concrete image that we watched from a bird's-eye view stood out as a clear indication of how education mediates the relationship between the state and children, making children in a sense not only their parents' children but also "children of the state." In his work on the invention of childhood, Philippe Ariès describes the process whereby children are separated from their parents, spend long days in school, and are subjected to the discipline of the state.

With the invention of schooling came our modern sense of the long childhood. Children would begin to be schooled for adulthood; it was no longer something you automatically picked up. "It inflicted on him the birch, the prison cell—in a word, the punishments usually reserved for convicts from the lowest strata of society. But this severity was the expression of a very different feeling from the old indifference: an obsessive love was to dominate society from the eighteenth century on. It is easy to see why this invasion of the public's sensibility by childhood should have resulted in the now better-known phenomena of Malthusianism or birth control" (Ariès [1960] 1996:397).

Philippe Ariès described the invention of childhood as related to changing patterns of family life in Europe; his insights seem to be relevant for the introduction of formal schooling in China at the turn of the century, although there are vital differences. A new understanding of the child emerged in Europe during the seventeenth century, and this new attentiveness to children was part of a story of modernity, whereby the child also became an object of discipline (Ariès [1960] 1996:397). According to Teresa Kuan, even though the idea of childhood became highly politicized in the post-Mao era, the discovery of childhood as a means for governing a nation happened a long time ago in Chinese history, at least as early as the consolidation of the Han dynasty (206 BC to AD 229). Educational institutions were established throughout the empire, as Confucian thinkers believed that moral education would serve as a more effective deterrent to crime than the strict laws and punishments of the Qin government (Kuan 2008:6). Canonical texts were identified and officially endorsed. One such text, *The Book of Rites*, which had originated in early antiquity, would serve as an authoritative source for educational theory and practice for the next two thousand years (Bai 2005:16, cited in Kuan 2008).[5]

It could be argued that in modern times in no other country has the connection between "obsessive love" and the disciplining of children through formal schooling been so pronounced. Whereas many countries view birth control as a means to accelerate modernization, China is the only country in the world that has made use of strict birth quotas (Fong 2004:3). Mao Zedong's plea to the population to have many children was replaced by Deng Xiaoping's new approach to shaping the body politic.[6] The parallel instigation of the one-child policy and the reopening of higher education created an environment in which drastic limitations placed on people's fertility went hand in hand with a renewed focus on educating the body politic. The result was the new educated person in China, who would both represent and create the progress of the nation.

Foucault's concept of governmentality can shed light on the Chinese notion of *guan*, meaning "to discipline, control, and administer" (Foucault 1977). The term refers to governing a state, but can also be applied to the education and disciplining of children. Children and young people in China are expected to be able to *guan* themselves. An inability to discipline oneself—*guan bu zhu ta ziji*—is thought to have catastrophic consequences, since doing well in school and, in particular, passing college entrance exams entail a great amount of discipline (Fong 2004:116). These exams provide a pivotal moment in young people's lives, which, as people often say, will determine a person's success in life. Foucault saw prisons and schools as analogous institutions, created to subject all individuals to the discipline of the state. Consider the following quote from Fong: "'Think of yourself as having entered a jail,' Xun Lu's father advised her when she enrolled at a college prep high school. 'From now on, you must focus entirely on your studies. Like a prisoner, you will not have any freedom to do things you enjoy. Your only hope is the trial, the college entrance exam, which will determine whether the rest of your life is joy or suffering'" (Fong 2004:115).

Significantly, however, the Chinese notion of *guan* also means "to care for, to take care of," as in *ta guan wo* ("he cares for me") or *ta bu guan wo* ("he does not care about/for me, he ignores me"). Thus *guan* is not only a form of discipline, but also a form of love and care. This form of care and control has a certain resemblance to the "obsessive love" that Philippe Ariès identified with the social invention of childhood. My focus here is on how young people struggle in various ways to experience themselves as autonomous people and try to come to terms with or distance themselves from the will of their parents, in particular their mothers and the parental state, sometimes uncannily termed a "stepmother."

The One-Child Policy and Higher Education

The one-child policy, introduced by Deng Xiaoping in 1979, had the aim not only of reducing the quantity of the population but also of improving its quality (*suzhi*) (Anagnost 2004:190). *Suzhi* 素质 is a compound of the characters *su* 素 and *zhi* 质 (Kipnis 2006:296–298). *Zhi* means "nature, character, or matter," whereas *su* has many meanings, including "unadorned, plain, white, and essence." Andrew Kipnis has clearly laid out a genealogy of the concept, showing that while the term used to be associated with inborn characteristics and eugenics, it has increasingly become linked with individual human qualities. The word *sushi*,[7] usually translated as "quality," has become central to Chinese governance. In other words, *suzhi* has connotations of what is worth striving for on the individual, familial, and social levels, although its meaning is far from clear. It marks hierarchies of high and low, rural and urban, educated and non-educated, modern and backward. Although my informants rarely referred to the concept of *suzhi*, it was well known to them and constituted an important backdrop to the competitive environment in which they lived and against which their aspirations for success and well-being came into focus.

The relationship between parents and the state has been described as an intergenerational contract (Milwertz 1997:133) in which the efforts of parents and the state go hand in hand to create a high-quality child. Good parents invest in the quality of their children, and in this way establish an ongoing reciprocal caring relationship. One of the incentives attached to one-child certificates in the early years of the one-child policy was that the only child was given priority when it came to entry into the best schools. But since practically all city district children are now only children, this is no longer the case, which means that competition for entry into the best schools and ultimately successful college enrollment is exceedingly fierce. The state encourages parents to take responsibility for the education of their children, posting slogans such as "Promote nine years of education, improve population quality" and "Nine years of hardship for parents is a lifetime of happiness for a child."

The dream of upward mobility through education has its roots in the imperial civil service exam system, a system of hierarchical selection that goes back more than a thousand years. Disrupted during the Mao era, the system was reinvented in the reform era (Fong 2004:101), with a critical change: whereas in imperial China, elite education was limited to male members of a small number of elite families, today both boys and girls from all sectors of society are told that they can climb the social ladder if they work hard enough and have the talent.

In the post-Mao era, the rearing of children and the education of young people became a topic of national concern, and the concerns of the state were often mirrored by parents. The reintroduction of the national college entrance examination (*gao kao*) in 1977 represented a fundamental rejection of the ideas of the Cultural Revolution. The desire for university degrees, referred to as "little red passports," was in sharp contrast to the previous emphasis on Mao's "little red book" of essential quotations. Academic talent, rather than political activism or class background, was to be the key to success within the new school system, focused on selecting and educating "talented people" with the resources needed to build a strong economy, rather than on spreading education equally to everyone (Thøgersen 2002:202). This has led to a situation in which practically all parents push their children to succeed in school—wishing their sons may turn into dragons (*wang zi cheng long*) who excel in life, even though they feel sorry about imposing such pressure on them. One father, dismayed at the way that children and young people are stuffed with knowledge, put it in this way: "We tell our children 'Eat! Eat! Eat!'—Even when they are full."

Since the 1980s, scholars have offered various and sometimes contradictory explanations for the debates that have revolved around the flaws of Chinese education. Drawing on, among other things, the American notion of "competence education" and ideas about the liberation of the student, some Chinese educators have used the "reform" language of the party. The term *suzhi jiaoyu*, which is usually translated as "education for quality," is extremely broad and encompasses changes in pedagogy, curricula, teacher training, and the structure of the educational system from kindergarten to university level (Woronov 2009:571).

Chinese top officials have declared that China now needs a new personality type in order to facilitate the transition to a knowledge society. This new vision is complex: the state promotes innovation while at the same time expecting conformity by limiting critical thinking and creativity to areas where political stability is not challenged. Furthermore, even though practically all of the Chinese people I met lamented the problems of education in China and agreed that students mostly learn for the sake of passing exams, they seemed equally skeptical about the ability of *suzhi jiaoyu* to have any real impact. Even though they longed for an alternative to *yingshi jiaoyu* ("test-based education"), they found that it was impossible to change the system, since tests are inevitably necessary in order to get to the next level within the system. The new emphasis on creativity and self-realization was also experienced as being at odds with the pressure to do well in exams, and for some students it was experienced as an additional source of pressure. Furthermore, some pointed out that even though test-based education had its flaws, at least it was in principle fair and equal for everybody.

My interlocutors belong to the lucky few who have made it to the top of the educational system, and yet all faced great expectations and a fear of falling behind. China's population of thirteen hundred million people is a dizzying number, along with other such statistics. Ten million middle-school students take the college entrance exam every year, and every child faces the problem of how to stand out from the crowd. As an example, an economics student at

Tsinghua University told me, "There were 20,000 applicants to my department and 200 were admitted. I was one of the top 10 best of my province."

How do young people experience being one in a million who have made it to the top of the educational system? What is the relationship between success and well-being? How do they experience and manage the tension between self-sacrifice and self-realization?

Self-sacrifice

"School means suffering—the more you suffer the more you can gain," Gu Wei, a student of economics, told me. But he had come to doubt that this was actually true. His comment illuminates how, as Andrew Kipnis poignantly put it, in China "education has become a mediating institution in a logic of sacrifice" (Kipnis 2009:210).[8]

Family sacrifice has a long history in China, and losses and gains are closely connected. This ethic is linked historically to the ideologies that interwove sacrificial ritual, state legitimacy, filial piety, and the teaching of literacy in late imperial China (Kipnis 2009:205).[9] One of the most important expressions of filial piety is diligent studying. As the old saying goes, "If there is no dark and dogged will, there will be no shining accomplishment: if there is no dull and determined effort, there will be no brilliant achievement." This saying is often invoked for the benefit of contemporary Chinese primary students and throughout the educational system (Hulbert 2007).

According to Marcel Mauss, every gift given demands a returned gift, so that gift giving creates a sense of indebtedness or obligation between people (Mauss [1925] 2006). Sacrifice is not a matter of giving up something for the common good, but is predicated on the expectation of some form of return (Jackson 2009:207). Hans Lucht has termed this phenomenon "existential reciprocity," pointing out that great suffering entails a sense that some reward lies in store—that there is always "darkness before daybreak" (Lucht 2012). This hopeful waiting is also captured in colloquial expressions such as "the fruits of our labor" or a "blessing in disguise," as well as the contrary "easy come, easy go."

But how does such a notion of sacrifice play out between generations? Who loses in order that someone else gains? During my fieldwork, I sometimes heard the dubious saying "China has changed from a society in which children serve their parents to a society in which parents serve their children." This ironic inversion of the notion of filial piety (*xiao*) or filial obligation came across as a clear expression of people's anxiety at the prospect of having a generation of "little emperors," reputedly spoiled and selfish, who might not be able to take care of their parents in the future. *Xiao*,[10] the moral obligation of children to honor and serve their parents, is a long-standing motif in Chinese life, and stories of children who cut off parts of their limbs in order to prepare a nourishing soup for their parents attest to the filial duty to sacrifice their own well-being for the sake of their parents' well-being (M. K. Whyte 1997).

This theme of reciprocity between the generations[11] takes on great significance in China today, as a generation of predominantly only children comes of age. With the breakdown of the cradle-to-grave social security provided in urban areas during socialism, no comprehensive system of support remains for the elderly. Therefore the desire to instill a sense of filial piety in this generation of young people is of great national concern. Acceptance of the one-child policy was tied to what has been described as an "informal contract" between parents and the state: by having only one child, who would grow up to become well-educated, parents could expect to see a paying back of the generational contract in the future (Milwertz 1997).

In contemporary China a child's schooling is a family endeavor involving great sacrifices, since it requires an investment of care, resources, and time. This is related to what Charles Stafford has called "the cycles of *yang*." *Yang* means "to give birth to," "to cultivate," "to educate," and "to nourish" (Stafford 1995:80). Parents' *yang* is to provide food, money, and care for their children, who will in time *yang* them when they grow old. Parents thus make sacrifices, in the sense of working hard to bring up their children, in the hope of making them succeed in a competitive society. For children, educational achievement is a means to make a return to parents, to repay *yang* (Stafford 1995:80). This relationship of mutual dependence is connected with the notion of *xiao*, filial piety. The Chinese educational system plays a substantial role in instilling this sense of indebtedness in children and young people.

From an early age Chinese primary students are taught to love and respect their parents, as well as Grandfather Hu, former president Hu Jintao. Children are also taught that their parents have made so many sacrifices that they must be given endless love (Kipnis 2009:216). For example, all grade six students have to memorize a Tang dynasty poem titled "Youzi Yin." It describes an old mother sewing clothes for her son by candlelight so that he can spend all his time studying and become an official in a faraway place. Students must memorize the poem so that they can read it aloud with feeling, imagine the sacrifices their parents have made to secure their education, and write essays about how they may repay their debt to their parents (Kipnis 2009:214). The moral obligation to repay the sacrifices made by one's parents thus works to create lifelong bonds between parents and children. In my view, human relationships, especially the relationship between parents and children, while bound by reciprocity, can never be thought of in *purely* contractual terms. As Marcel Mauss pointed out in relation to gift giving, the idea is never to give back the exact equivalent of what was given, for this would bring to an end the ongoing flow of reciprocity. Rather, a gift is reciprocated with a different gift and in this way retains a part of the giver in the form of the spirit or *hau* of the gift, which works to sustain social bonds or obligations between people (Mauss [1950] 2006:14–15).

Chinese students are taught not only to repay their parents' sacrifices, but also to make sacrifices to their country. According to Charles Stafford, some textbook stories depict virtuous mothers making sacrifices for the education of their sons, who as a result become great figures in Chinese history. One example is the story of Mencius:

"When Mengzi [Mencius] was young, his father died, and he thereafter lived with his mother. She felt he should receive a superior education [*lianghou de jiaoyu*] and thus paid careful attention to his surroundings. At first, they lived near a graveyard, and Mengzi watched as the bereaved buried their dead. When he was at play, he would imitate burials. Mother Meng felt this was inappropriate, and soon they left for another place. They then lived next to a slaughterhouse. There Mengzi watched as the pigs were killed, and when he played he imitated butchery. Mother Meng felt that this was also inappropriate, and they quickly moved again. Finally, they moved near to a school. Here Mengzi saw the people reading books, and he soon learnt to read. His mother felt this place would be good for her child, and they settled, no longer moving." (Stafford 1995:73)

The story highlights the idea of family sacrifices made in order to provide education, which is seen as the road to familial and national glory.

Students at Tsinghua University and Beijing University spoke both of the sacrifices their parents had made on their behalf, working hard so that they could get a university education, and of their own self-sacrifice, working diligently and eschewing play and leisure in order to bring about "a better life" for themselves and their families in the future. Only rarely did even party members talk about making sacrifices for their country.

Self-realization

One of my interlocutors, Ryan, was admitted to Tsinghua on special grounds, without having to take the ordinary college entrance examination (*gao kao*), since he had won the national physics competition. Knowing that this form of admittance was a form of *suzhi jiaoyu*, Ryan suggested that I should make sure to ask people in my interviews, "What makes you unique?" At the time, this question struck me as puzzling, and I did not systematically ask students any single question. But later, when working through my field notes, it became clear that many people were in fact very preoccupied with their own "uniqueness," and several students mentioned they were "quite unique," while others struggled to find ways to stand out from the crowd. This fetishizing of the individual is often assumed to characterize modernity in the affluent West, by contrast with the Orient, which is allegedly more self-sacrificial and observant of duty and tradition.

Existential anthropology rejects the idea that a person's humanity consists primarily in his or her *individual* will-to-be or self-realization.[12] When I use the term "self-realization" here, I am employing a colloquial term used by my interlocutors, for whom self-sacrifice seems to be held in tension with self-realization. These terms are not ontologies but should be seen as opposite extremes of imagined possibilities that my interlocutors in various ways strove to balance or reconcile. I see this struggle between self-sacrifice and self-actualization as part of a universal effort to experience a degree of determination over one's own destiny.

The "education for quality" movement (*suzhi jiaoyu*) has played a substantial role in shifting the ideal of education from a matter of rote memorization and cramming for exams to a focus on education as a form of self-development (*fazhan ziji*) or self-realization (*ziwo fazhan*) in which a person's *individual* qualities are nurtured. While this kind of rhetoric may echo Confucian notions of self-development or self-cultivation, what is new in contemporary China is that this is often conceptualized as involving a greater degree of self-determination. It is part of a national dream of fostering the same qualities that are believed to make Americans so successful. The notion of self-realization appeared frequently in my conversations with students, who often vacillated between describing education as a form of self-sacrifice and a form of self-realization. For some this was experienced as giving rise to a new form of pressure.

Let me return to the story of Mencius's mother. Chinese critics of contemporary education have questioned the sacrifice his mother makes by moving three times in order to enable her son to grow up in an appropriate environment surrounded by books and free from unnecessary worldly distractions. In a different reading, verging on the comical, of the famous story "Mencius' Mother Moves Three Times" (*Mengmu Sanqian*), one education critic writes:

"For the sake of her son's future, Mencius' mother moved three times. Of course she didn't consider whether or not Mencius wanted to leave his little companions, nor did she bother to ask his opinion, yet Mencius became China's greatest philosopher. In the thousands of years of the Chinese civilization, civilization was founded upon running-things-without-the-consultation-of-others (*baoban tidai*)" (Fu 2005:11, cited in Kuan 2008:158). This reading of the story seeks to change the authoritarian nature of the educational system and of parenting practices, which are seen as inhibiting the potential for "letting children flourish and achieve self-realization (*ziwo faxian*)" (Kuan 2008:158).

Along these lines, Yunxiang Yan argues that the phenomenal change that Chinese society has undergone in the last thirty years has been accompanied by the rise of the individual in both public and private spheres, and consequently by an *individualization* of Chinese society itself (2009). He notes the rapid changes in mentality and behavior among Chinese individuals who have increasingly demanded "the rights of self-development, happiness and security against the backdrop of age-old moral teachings of wellbeing" (Yan 2009:xvii). He describes the institutional reforms of the post-Mao era as part of a process in which young people in particular are now demanding their share of freedom, fulfillment, and self-determination (Yan 2009:127–129). In other words, Yan demonstrates that the new legitimacy of personal practices underlying group processes has fostered open expressions of self-interest that previously had to be articulated in collectivist terms to be publicly acceptable.

In this book I seek to describe the lives behind the policies of the state. I wish to describe the lived consequences of the one-child policy and its related educational ideals by looking at what it is like for different individuals to come of age under these specific historical conditions. The basic theoretical premise of the book is that human subjectivity is socially shaped. At different times individuality may be fetishized or downplayed, but this does not change the general human condition of striving to adjust oneself to the world as one finds it *and* live this world on one's own terms.

While my interlocutors stressed the necessity of self-sacrifice, they also spoke of a coexisting imperative or desire for self-development or self-realization. The latter is seen to imply something other than merely passing exams and being filial to parents, namely a sense of shaping their own destinies as well as a sense that sacrifices are rewarded. Students struggle in different ways to reconcile these contradictory social imperatives of self-sacrifice and self-realization, which can perhaps be seen as making up two contradictory yet interconnected paths or roads to adulthood.[13]

As the psychoanalytic anthropologist George Devereux has noted, every society has dominant and subdominant patterns, and at different historical epochs and within different individuals the dominant pattern may become background and the subdominant pattern[14] may emerge as foreground (Devereux 1967:212). In this way he pointed to the tension between what is publicly emphasized and what is publicly repressed, between dominant and subdominant ethical values and different modes of consciousness. As he noted, no societies are composed of individuals whose consciousness is entirely self-absorbed or entirely diffused into the collective. While the distinction between individualistic and sociocentric societies may hold true on the ideological plane, it is far from true when it comes to social practice.

Existential *Aporias*

In this book, I try to commit myself to a kind of anthropology in which people's experiences are never reducible to the social imperatives under which they live their lives, the policies they are affected by, or the social roles they feel more or less compelled to fit into or reject. My aim is to investigate how such struggles are negotiated and how people live their lives in the ethical space in between them (Jackson 2013). This is connected to an investigation of how my interlocutors struggle to increase their *being*, or a sense of a life worth living. I thus explore being not so much as a question of "either or" but as a question of "less or more" (Hage 2003:16). From a phenomenological point of view, I argue that education (*suzhi*) can be seen as what defines being at a particular point in history. The struggle for being may be understood "not as a fixed course, but as a course steered between a variable environment and the equally variable capacities of persons" (Jackson 1998:18–19)—in other words, as "the always uneven struggle of where the world is taking us and where we aspire to go" (Kleinman 2006:17).

Even though human beings always try to strategize in an attempt to "navigate" (Vigh 2003) and acquire a sense of "governing their own fate" (Jackson

1998:19), I focus on the instances in which it proves impossible to have it both ways. Gregory Bateson coined the term "double bind" to characterize the situation faced by a person who is receiving contradictory messages from another powerful person (Bateson [1972] 2000:271–279). The classic example is that of a child who is confronted with a parent who communicates withdrawal and coldness when the child approaches, but then reaches out toward the child with simulated love when he or she pulls back from the coldness. The child is then caught in a double bind; no course of action can possibly prove satisfactory. Bateson suggested that this kind of mixed communication might underlie the development of autism and schizophrenia. However, for my purpose it is necessary to clearly separate the notion of a double bind from any clinical content of this sort.

I see double binds as tied to *aporias*, that is, to moral quandaries that have no definite answer. *Aporia* literally means "lacking a path (*a- poros*), a path that is impassable" (Jackson 2007:xx). The classical Greek *aporia* was primarily a logical puzzle that was to be resolved through rational ingenuity.[15] In this book, the aim is to focus less on the *aporias* that arise from intellectual contemplation than on the existential dilemmas or double binds between self and other, as well as between moral ideals and lived experience (Jackson 2009:105). These dilemmas seem to be part of the human condition itself, and are related to universal themes of separation and attachment, dependency and autonomy that can be rephrased as the oedipal project.

"Chinese parents see their children as extensions of themselves," Zhou Lemin, a student of international relations at Tsinghua University, told me. "Chinese mothers constantly talk about the education of their *children*. This is the most important thing in their lives." He said that his mother is extremely proud of him now that he is a student of Tsinghua, but he recalled how he used to be so afraid of his mother, who would beat him with a stick when he did not study. He quoted Confucius: "If a son is not successful, it is the fault of the parents not the son." And he added that there is a saying that light will emanate from the house of a family whose children obtain a higher education.

By contrast, consider how Jimmy, a Tsinghua student of automation science, talked about his parents:

But you know, my parents are different from the typical Chinese government . . . I mean parents, sorry, typical Chinese parents always emphasize that you should go to the best high school, the best university, you should get a good job, earn a lot of money and lead a happy life. But my parents never said anything to me. I never knew what they were thinking. Unlike other parents, they never told me what they expected from me and they never rewarded me for doing well. I expect that they also had high expectations for me, but I was always disappointed that they never told me anything. When I came home from school and showed them my grades, they didn't say a word. I always expected that they were disappointed, but I never really knew.

He said that members of his parents' generation, who had had children during "the good and bad 1980s," had been very busy with their careers and had had very little time to look after their only children, who often grew up with either their grandparents or, in his case, in a state of loneliness. As for his own mother, who was a middle-school teacher, he recalled that she was often absent. She worked long days and never had weekends off.

You know in China, middle-school teachers are very busy. You know why? Because we have to educate our students so they can get into the best high schools and the best universities. So I was alone. Even now I don't communicate much with them. At least now I know that they are very proud that I have entered Tsinghua. They call me sometimes and ask about my health and my studying, but that is all.

Notice how Jimmy made the "Freudian slip" of saying "the government" (*zheng-fu*). Several students made this slip, indicating a certain blurring of boundaries between parents and the state in the minds of young people.

Both Zhou Lemin's and Jimmy's reflections also reveal the close association between parents/teachers and children/pupils. Zhou Lemin remembered the severe discipline and physical punishments of his mother as a kind of care, whereas Jimmy interpreted his parents' lack of explicit interest in his educational achievement as a sign of lack of love and affection. He suspected that they were disappointed but would have preferred to be told so or even to be punished, as opposed to being met with what he experienced as their lack of care. He seemed almost jealous of his mother's students, who had taken all her time and devotion. In this way he made a direct parallel between his mother's relationship to him as her son and the relationship she had to her pupils. Parental affection and discipline were thus conflated. A mother may be harsh, but discipline and care are better than indifference.

The instigation of the one-child policy entailed a critical transgression into the private sphere, in which the state controls women's bodies and restricts their desire to have more than one child. This was enacted through an informal contract between parents and the state; the promise was that this one child would grow up to become a child of high quality and in time repay the debt to the parents. As a result, pressure weighs heavily on the shoulders of China's youth.

Chapter 1

Sculpting in Time

> In serving his parents, a filial son reveres them in daily life; he makes them happy
> while he nourishes them; he takes anxious care of them in sickness; he shows great
> sorrow over their death; and he sacrifices to them with solemnity.
>
> —Confucius (551–479 BC), *Classic of Filial Piety*

ONE OF THE FIRST THINGS Jing Jing said to me was that she wanted to give her
mother a better life. I first met Jing Jing, a thirty-year-old Tsinghua University
law graduate during the spring of 2005, and as we sat together talking at a
French café called Sculpting in Time amid a crowd of loud students, she started
to cry and apologized for "wasting my time," since she felt that she could not go
through with the interview. She told me how her mother was not well. She had
worked hard as a primary school teacher in a small town in Yunnan province, in
order to raise two daughters on her own and had even sacrificed her own health
for her daughters, as she felt that receiving a higher education was the only way
for them to achieve a better life in the future. Jing Jing's tears, her agony over
being far away from her mother while she was ill, and her anxiety over being unable to repay her mother's sacrifices fit well into the cultural trope of filial duty.

It soon became clear, however, that Jing Jing's quandaries not only had to do
with wanting to give her mother a better life but also were tied to her own quest
for what I have called "self-realization." Coming from Yunnan province in the
poor western part of China, Jing Jing had made it to the top of the educational
ladder and had been accepted into an elite university in Beijing, an achievement
that many Chinese parents would see as the ultimate dream come true. Andrew
Kipnis (2011) has pointed out that parental desire for university education for
their children at times exceeds that of the state and has often become an end in
itself. However, in Jing Jing's case, her personal ambitions for acquiring a higher
education actually surpassed those of her parents. For Jing Jing, education was
more than a matter of finding a good job and being able to provide for her family. In a certain sense her ambitions matched the ideals of the "education for
quality" reforms (*suzhi jiaoyu*), which since the late 1980s have attempted to
create innovative, striving, and independent citizens, equal to their imagined
American counterparts (Woronov 2007). Having already graduated with a major

in English from the local university in Kunming, she had then taken a master's at the most prestigious university in the country, even though her mother had wanted her to remain closer to home. Jing Jing felt she was being torn in two directions, but she hoped that by acquiring a higher education, she would in time be able to repay her parents' sacrifice of the expensive tuition fees, and her dream was ultimately to bring her mother to Beijing so that Jing Jing could take care of her during her old age and enable her to live a happy life (*guo ri zi*).

However, although Jing Jing had graduated with a law degree from Tsinghua, she had been unable to find a job. Six months before our first meeting, she was still living in a small room erected temporarily for workers on campus, which was soon to be torn down. Next stop for Jing Jing would be finding a cheap apartment on the outskirts of Beijing in what Lian Si (2009) has termed "China's ant tribe"; the term refers to the millions of Chinese college graduates who have little or no employment and in many ways share the same fate and living conditions as the country's migrant workers. Describing how she would strenuously stretch her resources and shop for vegetables at a cheap market outside the campus, rather than spend money in the expensive canteens, she said, "Can you imagine? This is the life of a Tsinghua graduate." For Jing Jing, higher education had not provided the promised trajectory of social mobility, and as a result she was also unable to reverse the generational contract. As has been pointed out (Alber, van der Geest, and Whyte 2008), in many societies the uncertainties of how to go about the intergenerational contract are often the source of conflict. In China, time is the key to this relationship, since the ever-ambiguous question remains: when are the tables turned, and the young become responsible for caring for the old?

Under the Ancestor's Shadow?

Filial piety has long been recognized as one of the key moral concepts in Confucian ethics and one of the major principles structuring Chinese society (Weber and Parsons 1930; Freedman 1958; Tu 1985). In many scholarly accounts of China, family loyalty is seen as the overriding motif in Chinese life, and the consensus is that Chinese society is sociocentric in character, in sharp contrast to the individualistic orientation in Western societies. The work of anthropologist Maurice Freedman on Chinese kinship set the stage for this understanding of Chinese society, and has remained influential. Imperial society was understood to exist "under the ancestors' shadow" (Hsu 1967) and to be organized around familial ideals based on hierarchical relationships of age, generation, and gender (Brandstädter and Santos 2009). Following Freedman, "kinship" became strictly associated with descent, property, and lineage organization. In more recent ethnographies of China, however, the individual seems to have emerged from the ancestors' shadow.[1]

Let us now return to Jing Jing's family history and, by extension, to her relationship to the Chinese state.

. . .

It was not until we had met several times that I was really able to make sense of her story. Jing Jing told me in a low voice that her father had been in prison for twelve years. Up until this moment, Jing Jing's father had been more or less absent from her account, which had revolved around the difficulty of wanting to give her mother a better life while pursuing her own dream of higher education. Jing Jing took a notebook from her bag and carefully unfolded a piece of paper. She explained that in order for me to understand her situation, it was necessary for her to tell a longer story. It turned out that she had copied down part of an inscription from the family shrine that had been inaugurated in 1947 in her hometown. As we had coffee off-campus at a theme park-like café decorated in the style of a Swiss alpine cottage, I was struck that Jing Jing's account of her family genealogy transported me to an utterly different time and place. I listened and took notes as she meticulously translated the following from the family shrine of her mother's patrilineal descent line, starting with her great-great-grandfather:

Jiao's family originated from Nanjing. At the end of the Ming dynasty (1368–1644) it settled in Yunnan province and lived there for generations. Jiao Wenjia married a young girl with the family name of Yang. They had four sons and five daughters [the names of the sons are listed]. They focused all their energy and resources on education, and the children grew up to become successful. The third son, Lian Zhu, was generous and smart and particularly fond of studying. When he was twenty he was appointed to the office in charge of regional affairs in Zhi Li in Sichuan province. Several years later, during the revolution led by Sun Yatsen [in 1911], he came back to Yunnan province and worked for the civil and treasury department of the province. Later he was appointed to be a member of the bank inspectorate of the province, and he traveled throughout the entire province. Later he became the manager of the Bank of Fudian at Shi Ping. In 1915 he became the manager of Yong Chan (now known as Bao Shan).

In 1923 he moved to Burma as a manager and acquired a glorious reputation. In 1929 he felt that his health had become fragile, and he resigned from his position and returned to Yunnan to educate his sons. He was very devoted to Buddhism and built a monastery. He acquired scriptures to be sent from Suzhou and Hangzhou (and because of this, Buddhism is still widely practiced in Tao Jian). Here he diligently studied the classics, both Buddhism and Confucianism. He lived in a stoic way and was famed for his devotion to helping others in need. In his family he respected his father and his elders, and in his work he was a person of his word. He was also very capable in mediating in disputes. Therefore he was widely respected in the region. Lian Zhu put strong emphasis on education. He thought that "A person cannot not study, a home cannot not be educated, study to become accomplished, teach with effort. Without education, having sons is like not having sons, having a home is like not having a home."

Although he was very preoccupied with his work at the monastery, he educated his sons day and night and invested a lot in their education with a view to "look from a high place and see far away," "sparing no effort." *Jia wei* [Confucian term for the educational status of the home] was built up, and in the following decades his sons all made great achievements within their families and for the country. His wife was named Li, and she supported her husband by taking care of the home. They had five sons and two daughters [the names of the sons are listed]. The first son, Shu [Jing Jing's grandfather] graduated from the National South East University of Nanjing. Two years later he went to America and got a master's degree from the University of Michigan. When he returned to China he was appointed to a key position within the nationalist Guomindang government.[2]

The account is paradigmatic in describing traditional Chinese society as characterized by the subordination of the young and of women to the dominant patriarchal ideology and power structure as well as in its equation between education and moral personhood. However, what is notable is that Jing Jing told me the story of her mother's ancestors, not her *father's* patriline, and that she took for granted that she and her mother ought to have been given the same opportunities for education and self-development as her male ancestors. Whereas in imperial China, elite education was limited to male members of a relatively small number of elite families, today both boys and girls from all sectors of society are told that they can climb the social ladder if they work hard enough and have the talent (Fong 2004, 2011).

And yet merely identifying the societal structures did not seem like a satisfactory way of doing justice to her story. Why did Jing Jing choose to narrate this long tale to me, a foreigner and a near stranger? Did she intend to validate her choice to gain higher education through the moral standing that her (male) ancestors had obtained through higher education? By showing me her mother's patrilineal descent line, rather than the descent line of her own father, was she emphasizing her connectedness with her mother and trying to evict her father from her life? Or did she aim to address the political injustice that befell her family after the 1949 revolution, as this links up with her desire to study law and work toward a more just society?

1949

Jing Jing herself took up the story where the family shrine's account had left off. She went on to tell me of the tragic turning point in her family history when her grandfather entered the Guomindang. The iconoclasm of the 1949 revolution involved an attack on old ideas, old values, and bourgeois education. The class categories were to be overturned and the "new man of socialism" was to be created. During the Cultural Revolution (1966–1976) her grandfather was forced to perform "self-criticism." In a staged performance peasants gathered at twilight to watch the confessions of the previous ruling classes and the intelligentsia, who were labeled "rightists," "revisionists," and "black elements." Their houses were confiscated, and any items that did not conform to Mao's values were smashed. Jing Jing said that after her grandfather's death she had found his diary, in which he had described the degradation and humiliation of the physical and spiritual torture he had been subjected to. As a result of her grandfather's political status, Jing Jing's mother was bullied by her peers as a child, as well as by some of her teachers.

Jing Jing's mother fell in love with the son of a landlord. However, because of her unfortunate class status, she was forced to marry someone with a "better" background—that is, someone who did not belong to the bourgeois class. Her parents arranged that she be married to Chen, Jing Jing's father, since he had a peasant background and was a devoted revolutionary. Jing Jing's mother had no choice but to agree to the marriage. And yet she seemed to stumble into one catastrophe after another; while her husband's status was intended to salvage her fate, it actually caused her great suffering when he was imprisoned after the end of the Cultural Revolution. After Deng Xiaoping came to power, Jing Jing's father was imprisoned because he belonged to the Mao faction and the political tide had changed. Jing Jing told me her father served twelve years in prison as a scapegoat for other people's crimes. He was sentenced in 1978 when she was only three years old. She remembered her older sister cursing the public loudspeakers of the village when the sentence was announced. For years her mother had tried to have his sentence reversed, but with no success. "In China this in reality means asking for mercy, since the government would never admit to having been wrong," Jing Jing said.

In 1990, Jing Jing's father was released from prison. His release occurred during the stressful period leading up to Jing Jing's college entrance exams. Jing Jing's father was thirty years old when he was imprisoned, and he was forty-two when he was released. According to Jing Jing, the imprisonment had made him bitter, and he took his anger out on Jing Jing's mother. Due to the situation at home Jing Jing was unable to concentrate on her studies. She despised the way her father, whom she had never really known, acted unreasonably while presenting himself as if he were a hero. Due to the violent conflict between her parents and the pressure of having to take the college entrance exams, Jing Jing attempted to run away from home several times, and she also attempted suicide. After Jing Jing's failed suicide attempt, her mother had performed a kow-tow (*ketou*), a ritual display of filial piety whereby a young person kneels before his or her ancestors. As Jing Jing's mother begged her daughter never to attempt to take her own life again, she was reversing the relationship between parent and child, and Jing Jing remembers this inversion of filial piety as the most harrowing experience of her life.

Jing Jing then failed the college entrance exams, but as a result of her mother's ability to persuade and bribe local officials, she was allowed to take the exams the following year. She passed the test this time but did not get a very high score and was admitted to the Yunnan Nationalities University in Kunming, where she took a master's degree in English and received one of the highest grades in the university. However, Jing Jing felt that the level of education there was low, and after graduation she applied to the law school of Tsinghua University in Beijing and was accepted from among thousands of other applicants. Because of her father's unfair trial and an acute awareness of the injustice of society, she was attracted to the idea of studying law and ultimately working for a more just system. Although her mother had always urged her to acquire a higher education, her mother found these ambitions dangerous and naive and now she urged her daughter to stay closer to home and to lead "a quiet life," by which she meant getting married and having a child. We can recall that Jing Jing wanted to pursue a higher education in order to "learn more and experience more in life," as well as to find a good job and help her mother live a better life, while at the same time feeling guilt and self-reproach since her decision meant being thousands of miles away from her mother at a time when her mother needed her most.

Jing Jing did manage to persuade her mother to let her pursue her own dream of higher education, and so she traveled to Beijing, a two-day train ride from her hometown, and became a student at the most prestigious university in the country. However, when she returned home during the Spring Festival to visit her family during her first year, she discovered that her mother was not well. The family had kept this a secret in order not to worry her and to enable her to focus on her studies. She felt responsible for her mother's poor health because she had left her alone with her father, who had acted tyrannically and even physically abused her. When her mother was periodically hospitalized, Jing Jing's sister visited her as often as she could, but she had also moved to the capital of the province, and therefore Jing Jing's mother mostly had to depend on her husband. In China, when people are hospitalized, it is customary that a person's family plays a substantial role in their treatment through practices of *yang*: providing food, linen, and washing the patient, as well as providing care and company. Her mother's illness happened at a point where Jing Jing was under the pressure of having to take several important exams, and she found herself being consumed by worries about her mother. The exam process itself was highly stressful, requiring the memorization of vast amounts of information, reminding her of her college entrance exams. She described the feeling that she was choking on information, and spoke of her struggle to make what she had read stick in her mind. This experience was far from her dream of obtaining a more highly developed understanding of Chinese society and in the process being transformed as a person. Jing Jing described desperately needing someone to talk to. Although she was sharing a dormitory with several girls, she found that the difference in their backgrounds, as well as an element of competition among them, made it impossible for her really to express her feelings to them.

At some point, Jing Jing contacted one of her teachers, who she felt genuinely *cared* about her well-being. However, she did not find the experience helpful. In some ways, the teacher only exacerbated Jing Jing's experience of being torn in two directions; she told Jing Jing that her preoccupation with her mother's well-being was crucial, and at the same time urged her to concentrate on her studies in order to be able to manage the upcoming exams. Jing Jing came to regret that in her view she had imposed her problems on her teacher, and worried whether her act of confiding in her teacher would in any way compromise her academic standing.

Jing Jing felt guilty about being far away from home. She also felt guilty that her parents and sister were sending her money to enable her to continue studying, which would otherwise have been used for her mother's treatment. However, she continued to cling to the hope that by obtaining a good education she would eventually be able to help her mother live a better life in her old age. It is therefore easy to understand her desperation when her aspirations seemed to fail and she was unable to find a job after graduation.

It seemed as if Jing Jing's social status was blocking the road of upward mobility, despite her talent, hard work, and Tsinghua diploma. She suspected that the reason she was being bypassed when applying for positions as a civil servant was to be found in her *dang an*, the personal dossier of every Chinese citizen, which contains details of a person's family record. In other words, she suspected that it was her father's prison sentence that was exerting power over her life. Her road toward social mobility and adulthood was therefore blocked. She spoke of the discrimination of the labor market by referring to the popular phrase *bei nan dang*, a term implying that success comes more easily if one is from Beijing (**bei** jing), is a man (**nan** shi), and is a member of the Communist Party (**dang** yuan). As a Dao minority woman with a convicted father and no personal connections, she seemed to be jinxed.

About a year later everything had taken a turn for the better. Jing Jing had married and found a job at a foreign company in Beijing. Having spent the Spring Festival nurturing her husband's family, "which was expected," she said, Jing Jing and her husband were happily preparing a room in their apartment for the arrival of Jing Jing's mother, who was to come and live with them. The idea was also that Jing Jing's mother should look after the child they hoped to have in the future.

Jing Jing's Double Bind

Jing Jing's hopes for her mother were not realized. Soon after I returned to Beijing in February 2007 to continue fieldwork, I received the news that Jing Jing's mother had passed away. She had never fully recovered from her illness and she had never made it to Beijing. Jing Jing had spent several months taking care of her in her hometown. Because Jing Jing had been away from her job for such a long time, she had been fired. She was depressed and asked me to forgive her for not wanting to see me or anybody else at this point. After some time she sent me a poem by a Han dynasty poet, Han Ying (180–157 BC), taken from the *Book of Songs*, which is said to have been compiled by Confucius himself:

The tree may wish to be calm,
but the wind will not subside.
The son wants to take care of his parents,
but the parents are no longer there.

树欲静而风不止
子欲养而亲不在

The poem mirrors her experience of losing her footing when she was deprived of the possibility of taking care of her mother during her old age and in a state of bereavement. Even though Jing Jing had spent several months looking after her mother during her terminal illness, she was full of self-reproach, regretting having spent time on her own further education at Tsinghua and neglecting what she saw as her moral responsibility to take care of her mother during the last years of her life. She blamed herself for having made the wrong decision when she chose education as the most important thing in life, which led her to abandon her mother at a critical time after her father had been released from jail. This brings to mind Hannah Arendt's ([1958] 1998) distinction between *vita activa* and *vita contemplativa*, between life as it is chaotically lived and the way in which we make post hoc rationalizations of the events that befall us. Arendt emphasizes that human action always involves more than the singular subject because it occurs within a field of social relations, or what she calls "the subjective in-between." In this way she quite radically argues against the idea of an intentional actor, saying that human existence happens in the indeterminate space *between* actors. This approach finds resonance in the Taoist image of a small human being on a boat between two towering cliffs. The person has an oar to steer with, but the force of the river places a limit on his ability to navigate. It also evokes the vernacular expression that Chinese society/history is a "tide" that sweeps across people's lives with dramatic, sometimes devastating results. The expression certainly seems to apply to the lives of Jing Jing's grandfather and parents. The poem Jing Jing sent me about the tree that is at the mercy of external forces can be seen as expressing a similar experience. As Jackson points out, such a view is not to be mistaken for the kind of fatalism or determinism that the West so often ascribes to the East. People everywhere do the best they can in whatever circumstances they find themselves, but we do not necessarily know *what* we are doing *when* we are acting (Jackson 2007, 2013).

Jing Jing's wish to be a filial daughter proved to be at odds with her wish to live out her own desires. In relation to the Chinese state, it is worth noticing, Jing Jing's desires for self-realization and striving for higher education in a highly independent way in theory correspond to the ideals of "education for quality" that promote independence, critical thinking, and innovation rather than merely cramming for the sake of passing exams. However, in practice, higher education seemed largely devoid of real meaning to Jing Jing, and her story indicated that doing well at university in practice meant sticking to book learning and conformity, leaving no room for critical thinking or a quest for societal justice.

Even though Jing Jing was uncertain about her choice to go to Beijing for further education when she simultaneously felt an obligation to be at home and to be able to take care of her mother, she hoped that by acquiring a higher education she could eventually "give her mother a good life" by bringing her to Beijing. But time ran out. In other words, I think her case shows that her desire for self-realization in the form of living out her dream of obtaining a higher education and wanting to "experience more in life" does not mean that her sense of obligation to look after her mother was not equally strong. The two imperatives of self-realization and self-sacrifice coexisted and could not be separated even if, in practice, she was unable to realize both.

Jing Jing's mother died before Jing Jing was able to reverse the generational contract. She later told me that the fact that her mother had passed away also meant she was vexed about the issue of having a child. She could not see how having a child could be reconciled with her desire to work now that her mother was no longer there to do the caretaking. This conflict highlights the dilemma between the need to nurture others and the need to nurture one's own dreams and desires. In Jing Jing's case, her remorse for having put her own education ahead of her mother's welfare subsequently translated into her guilt about putting her own needs above the potential needs of her child.

Perspectives

By re-telling the story Jing Jing told me, I do not intend to portray her as a victim worthy of our pity. Rather, as Hannah Arendt has brilliantly put it, whereas pity is a perverted form of compassion, which creates a sentimental distance between oneself and the suffering other, compassion, not unlike love, entails seeing the other as ourselves in other circumstances (Arendt 1963). Similarly, I have wanted to avoid generalizing tropes such as individualism and collectivism in order to show that both perspectives, although contradictory, coexist. Every society has dominant and subdominant patterns, and in different historical epochs and within certain individuals the dominant pattern may become background and the subdominant pattern may emerge as foreground (Devereux 1967). In this way Jing Jing experienced a tension between what could be emphasized most clearly, namely her willingness to bear sacrifices for her mother, and what was publicly repressed, her own desires as well as her sense of political disillusionment. She struggled to negotiate contradictory social imperatives while being subjected to social forces largely out of her control.

And yet, having explored intergenerational reciprocity as tied to an idea of sacrifice, we see that sacrifice and self-interest are not entirely oppositional terms. The factor of time must also be taken into account. Arthur Kleinman and Joan Kleinman (1996) have called the generation of Jing Jing's mother, who had their years of education disrupted by the Cultural Revolution, a "lost generation." In effect, the Chinese state has written this generation off and is instead concentrating on the next generation. At stake here is also the fact that when the members of this "lost generation" place their own (lost) aspirations on their children, it is not only a form of self-sacrifice but also a way of giving meaning to their own lives, through their children. It is also connected to the desire to secure children's filial obligations so that the children will take care of the parents in the future. With regard to Jing Jing, it turned out that the desire to give her mother a good life during her old age was also connected to a desire that she could at the same time take care of the child she and her husband hoped to have. Again sacrifice and self-interest were intimately connected.

With the contemporary strong focus on higher education, those who make it to the top of the educational ladder remain in the period of youth longer than young people with less education do. They remain dependent on their parents for a longer period of time, as it takes longer for them to graduate, marry, and set up their own households. Jing Jing now regrets the choices she made and thinks that if she had remained content with her master's degree from the university in Kunming, she could perhaps have married, found a job near her natal village, and looked after her mother. But having higher aspirations, she wanted to take another degree at a better university, and in doing so she delayed the inversion of the generational contract further. In Jing Jing's case, prolonged education as well as her mother's early death made the expected inversion of the generational contract impossible, meaning that she was unable to grow up in a moral sense. The gift of life remains unpaid and continues to haunt her. Furthermore, she cannot see how she can have a child now that her mother is not there to take care of it, and thus she is not sure how to continue the family line. Like Jing Jing, the students I interviewed were unilateral in their conviction that it was their responsibility to look after their parents in their old age. This responsibility is most clearly felt by students from rural or poor backgrounds, but all students regard care of their parents in old age as their duty. However, unlike Jing Jing, most of my interlocutors had not yet graduated, and thus this was not as yet a practical concern to them.

Jing Jing's perspective placed her in a double bind, or a situation in which it was impossible to "have it both ways." When she traveled to Beijing to acquire a higher education and cried because she recognized her mother's sacrifice that had made this possible, she was in a sense enacting the role of the "son" in the Tang dynasty poem memorized by Chinese primary students that I mentioned in the introduction. For Jing Jing, acquiring a higher education was not only a matter of living up to family and state ideals; it was also an attempt to come into her own. However, this does not mean that living up to family obligations and reciprocating the generational contract were not equally important to her, and therefore she was full of guilt and remorse. Perhaps this is why she chose to tell me her story. It is possible that she saw me as someone who would validate her choice to pursue her own dreams rather than be constrained by a sense of family loyalty. In this way, her story illustrates the tensions in the Chinese modernity project and the contradictory demands that the present generation of young people will in different ways and to different degrees eventually face at some point in their lives.

As for loyalty to the state, in Jing Jing's case higher education had produced a certain measure of upward social mobility, but it had not fostered a sense of loyalty to the state or to the Chinese Communist Party (CCP). Rather, she felt that higher education was lacking in the capacity to address real-life situations when it came to law and that the Chinese judicial system was full of flaws and corruption. She had thought that entering the school of law at Tsinghua University would mean access to the highest forms of learning. However, she was now greatly disappointed to find that rather than pursuing justice or wanting to work toward creating a better society, most of her peers were keen to make money. Furthermore, several job advertisements within the state bureaucracy required applicants to be members of the CCP and Jing Jing did not believe this was an option available to her, because of her father's criminal record. Neither did she really want to go down that path, she said.

When I was last in contact with Jing Jing, she was still mourning the double life she could not lead and regretting the road she had taken. I wrote to her to tell her that I am quite sure that her mother would not want her to feel guilty for the rest of her life but would prefer her to be happy and to move on with her own life. If she had remained in Kunming, she might have regretted the road she had not taken. When I recently sent her an e-mail message, I found myself in a quandary as to whether my main motive for writing to her was a concern for her well-being or a desire to give my own story a happy ending. Moreover, how could I justify it as being a matter of both? I am still hoping that she will write back soon to tell me that she now sees things differently, that she has found a job and a way to have a child after all, and that this could be a new beginning.

Chapter 2

Filial Piety and Existential Dilemmas

XIAO YU TOLD ME that she remembered seeing her mother for the first time at Beijing International Airport, when she was four years old. Her grandmother told her that this was her mother, but she saw a stranger standing in front of her. When Xiao Yu's parents migrated to the United States in the 1980s in search of higher education as part of what has been called the *chu guo chao* ("wave/exodus from the country"), they left her to grow up with her grandparents. They later found work in American academia, and since then she had seen them once a year, during the summer holidays. In this way they had also been able to evade the one-child policy and have another child, a baby boy. When she referred to her "parents," she actually meant her grandparents. "To me they are my parents," she said. She spoke very fondly of them but also said that they did not communicate so much. They had always been rather strict, urging her to study and not to waste too much time playing, but now as she lived her life independently at Tsinghua University, she nostalgically longed for the comfort of home, her grandmother's good cooking and the quiet company of her grandfather.

I was moved by her story and found her reluctance to talk about her mother understandable, and yet it stood out in stark contrast to how most students talked about their parents. Students' stories often revolved around their relationship with their mothers, while their fathers tended to be more in the background, or absent altogether.

Years after, I can clearly picture Xiao Yu's doll-like face, her cautious eyes, and the way she spoke fluent English in a voice that had a childlike quality to it. Since she had done so well in school, she had skipped two grades in secondary school and was now younger than her classmates, only nineteen years old. Xiao Yu said that she missed her grandparents and that she was also worried about them. "They are old," she said, and "their health is getting poorer." Her grandfather had high blood pressure, and she was worried that he was not taking his doctors' advice to change his diet seriously enough. It was hard for him to change his habits, she said. She spoke fondly of her biological father, but her mother was always absent from her accounts. She proudly showed me pictures of her cute little brother, whom she also missed, she said.

Xiao Yu's biological father had told her about the time he used to work in a factory during the Cultural Revolution and how he secretly spent his spare time reading books. He and her mother belonged to the generation that was allowed to take the reopened college entrance exams at a later age, and they found that they were lagging behind their younger classmates, so they had worked diligently ever since to catch up. Xiao Yu's father always urged her to seize the opportunity to work hard and acquire a good education. Xiao Yu was studying automation science, which was also her father's major, and when I asked her about this choice of topic, she said, "I usually agree with my father and so we are very happy!"

But she seemed far from happy. She recalled the previous year, when she had started her university studies and moved into her dormitory at Tsinghua, as a difficult time. "I used to miss my parents [i.e., grandparents] a lot. I found living on campus very uncomfortable. I didn't like the food and I wasn't used to having to take care of so many things myself. Life in high school is really simple. All you have to do is study. Living here is much more complicated. You have to manage your own time, clean your clothes, handle social relationships."

When I asked her whether she experienced a generation gap in relation to her grandparents, she said that her grandparents were worried that she might be naive and become involved in a relationship in which she would be taken advantage of. However, she emphasized that she was not interested in boys or in having a boyfriend. To her it was more important to obtain a good education, and she was not even sure that she wanted to get married in the future. When she looked at the relationship between her biological parents, she found it hard to believe in marriage, she said.

Over the course of our conversations, I got the clear impression that Xiao Yu in no way contested the will of her parents and grandparents, describing it as congruent with her own, "and so we are very happy." However, I could not help wondering whether she was in a sense blocked from growing up and really coming into her own. It struck me that her seeming reluctance to grow up might have been connected with her fear of losing her aging grandparents.

In any case, the somewhat infantile impression Xiao Yu made on me brings to mind a quote from the work of George Devereux: "If I remain a child forever, if my very existence continues to depend on the presence of my parents, I can arrest the progress of time. By staying a child, I prevent my parents from becoming old and dying. If I am a dependent child, they simply have neither the right, not even the possibility of deserting me by dying" (Devereux 1958:185). As I see it, Xiao Yu's story highlights the relationship between existential power and time. My point here is that this is accentuated by the fact that her "parents" are actually her grandparents and thus she is acutely aware that it is most likely that they will die before her biological parents do. Xiao Yu longed for the infantile protection and care of "home," which made up her sense of "ontological security," because her biological parents had in a sense abandoned her for a life and careers abroad, bringing up their American Chinese son there.

Oedipal Stories

> Lao Lai-tzu was a man of the country of Ch'u. When he was 70 years old, his parents were still alive. His filial piety was very strong. Constantly clothed in a medley of garments [like children], when he carried drink to his parents, he pretended to stumble on arriving at the hall, then remained lying on the ground, uttering cries after the manner of little children. Or else, with the object of rejuvenating his old parents, he remained before them playing with his long sleeves, or amusing himself with chickens.
>
> —Devereux 1964:185, cited in Jackson 2006:219

> If in the fantasy of early growth, there is contained death, then at adolescence there is contained murder . . . because growing up means taking the parents' place. It really does. In the unconscious fantasy, growing up is an inherently aggressive act.
>
> —Winnicott 1974:169

The famous story about Lao Lai-tzu can be seen as a caricature of filial obedience. Filial piety defines a son's agency to be an extension of his father's, and Lao Lai-tzu remained childish to please and rejuvenate his parents, conveying the moral obligation of a child to be filial toward his or her parents, who have given him or her the gift of life. It is only when his father becomes an ancestor, no longer possessing desires and agency of his own, that the son can assert himself fully as owner of his own intentions (Sangren 1987:118). In this way the story is an example of a blocked oedipal project or a story of prevented succession. In the educational system, Chinese students are taught different versions of this story: "*Xiao* (filial obedience) applies to men and women, regardless of age; everyone must be utterly *xiao* to their parents. For example, Lao Laizi, over seventy years old, wishing his parents to be happy, often wore brightly coloured garments and practiced children's singing and dancing, in order to amuse his parents" (*Shenghuo yu lunli*, 6:27, cited in Stafford 1995:29). Here there is a denial of the passage of time, which prevents Lao Laizi from growing up and becoming an independent person.

The ambiguous character of parent–child relationships and the quandaries of intergenerational succession are powerfully expressed in oedipal stories, in which are played out the existential imperative of a child to grow up and come into his or her own (Brown 1959:118; Jackson 2006:217). The Confucian notion of filial obligation can be seen as a variation of this universal theme. But whereas in the classic Oedipus myth the son unwittingly kills his father, and in the Freudian interpretation of the myth, patricide is a hidden desire of a son as he obtains maturity and independence, in the stories of filial obligation the child by contrast sacrifices his own well-being for the parent. Filial obligation implies that children should be loyal and obedient to their parents, who have given them the gift of life. *The 24 Paragons of Filial Piety* contains an exemplary story of filial piety. During the Jin dynasty there was a son named Wu Meng, born to a family that was too poor to own a mosquito net. When the sting of mosquitoes made it difficult for his family to sleep, Wu Meng took off his shirt and sat by his parents' bed, letting the mosquitoes bite him rather than his parents. While China's imperial dynasties stressed loyalty to one's ruler and country alongside loyalty to one's parents, during the Cultural Revolution the *24 Paragons of Filial Piety* was banned as part of an attempt to replace family loyalty with loyalty to the Chinese Communist Party. However, since the reform era, the CCP has increasingly begun to promote filial piety, so that once again loyalty to parents should go hand in hand with loyalty to the party.

Steven Sangren has pointed out that the oedipal tensions that are at the heart of family life in China have traditionally played out differently depending on one's gendered vantage point. Through analyzing the story of Nezha from the Ming epic *Fengshen Yanyin* (*Investiture of the Gods*) and the story of the Princess Miaoshan, he argues that even though the dilemma of autonomy and separation is universally implicated in the development of intimate social relationships, the social organization of Chinese family life substantially differentiates sons' and daughters' experiences of these dilemmas (Sangren 1987:105). Daughters are destined to separate by marrying out of their natal families, and thus from the perspective of their natal families they are like "spilled water." In contrast, sons cannot escape patrilineal continuity since "they are its embodied realization." The Nezha story centers on a son's desire to establish his autonomy from his father and to distance himself from his *unchosen* role in establishing patrilineal continuity, while the story of Miaoshan relates a daughter's defiant rejection of her father's wish that she marry.

In this way oedipal myths abound in many versions across both societies and time. Meyer Fortes showed how the decline and death of the father is sometimes thought to be organically linked to the rising power of the first-born son, as among the Tallensi of northern Ghana, who hold that an "inborn antagonism" exists between the *yin* (individual destiny) of a father and the *yin* of his oldest son (Fortes 1949:227). Among the Kuranko of Sierra Leone, stories of prevented succession and delayed conception can be seen as attempts to annul time, thus preventing the young from replacing the old (Jackson 2006:191). As Fortes pointed out, close kinship ties involve *both* hostility and love, rivalry and solidarity, and the relationship between parents and their children in time involves children taking their parents' place (Fortes [1959] 1981:269).[1] According to Fortes:

The crucial feature is the conjunction of successive generations in the relationship of parents and their children, and this[,] it is obvious, comes into existence, once and for all, with the birth of the first child. Multiplying offspring produces the sibling group and thus makes a parent, perhaps, more of a parent in a quantitative sense: but it only builds on, it does not generate the condition and status of parenthood. (Fortes 1959:219)

Fortes argues that the firstborn therefore holds a central place in all human societies, as it generates the status of parenthood and thus is invested with religious, as well as legal, moral, and political meaning.

If we are to believe Meyer Fortes that it is the firstborn child who initiates the status of parenthood, then it also seems likely that having only one child/being an only child is a defining characteristic of this relationship and that this structural position is fraught with considerable ambiguity for both the parents and the child. To paraphrase Vanessa Fong, Chinese singletons are the "only hope" of their parents (Fong 2004). This is not to say that issues of gender are irrelevant, but that to a large extent similar expectations are placed on boys and girls, in particular in urban China, where the one-child policy is much more vigorously enforced.

The Oedipal Project

In order for the notion of the Oedipus complex to have cross-cultural relevance, it is necessary to rephrase it in terms of an existential imperative to find a balance between self and other. Norman Brown reconstructed Freud's notion of the Oedipus complex as the "oedipal project" in order to highlight the existential need for a child to separate from his or her parents in order to become an independent person. Accordingly, he emphasizes a process whereby a person moves from being a passive object of fate, dependent upon the parents, to being an active master of his or her social world (Brown [1959] 1989:118). In order to avoid ethnocentrism, it is important to free the notion of the Oedipus complex from its Freudian emphasis on the "narrowly sexual issues of lust and competitiveness" (Jackson 2006:217). As existential psychoanalysts argue, what is universal about the oedipal project is the imperative desire to negotiate one's own will in relation to one's parents and the social world of others (Brown [1959] 1989).

In other words, the oedipal project implies a universal struggle between parental determination and self-determination. The child is able to grow up and become an independent person only through some sort of denial of the will of the parent(s). This transition to independence is painful for both parents and children, since many children may be reluctant to give up the security their parents have given them, while the parents may find it traumatic to give up the meaning that their status as parents has given them, which also entails facing their own mortality. As Michael Jackson points out, this process of becoming a person in one's own right is never fully achieved, since the yearning to become independent is countermanded by a desire for dependency. Or, as Jing Jing's story so clearly conveys, the desire to do what one wants is no less urgent than the desire for limits, and the dream of a more fulfilling life comes up against one's sense of obligation and indebtedness to others. When the migrant wishes to create a new life elsewhere, the price may be a painful separation from primary bonds and a sense of not living up to the moral obligation to care for one's parents. For Jing Jing, this meant suffering guilt and remorse—a kind of survivor guilt. One can only speculate as to whether or not Xiao Yu's parents' new life in the United States also entailed guilt—at having abandoned their daughter.

Similar dilemmas face China's millions of migrant workers who move to big cities in search of employment, often leaving their children behind in their natal villages, to grow up with grandparents. Lixin Fan's documentary *Last Train Home* powerfully focuses on the dilemmas of one such family. The film portrays the world's largest migration, which takes place at the lunar New Year (also known as the Spring Festival) when 130 million workers return from China's industrial cities to their homes in the countryside. The film tells the story of a married couple who "harden their hearts" in order to leave their children behind and take up work in Guangzhou. They see this as a necessary sacrifice in order to make the money needed to provide for the family and bring prosperity to the next generation. After many delays, the parents finally return home for a visit, but parents and children are painfully estranged from each other. The children, who are at this point teenagers, are full of remorse and feel abandoned by their parents, and the parents are shocked to find that their oldest daughter is planning to drop out of school and migrate to a large city in search of work. The parents have sacrificed so much in order for their children to have a different and better life that they cannot bear the prospect of their sacrifices not paying off, or not leading to social mobility for the next generation. However, the daughter blames her parents for caring only about money, and refers to school as the equivalent of being in prison. When she refuses to listen to her parents (and grandparents), things go from bad to worse, and finally the whole family get into a heated argument, which culminates in the daughter's swearing rudely at her father. This loss of face is more than he can bear. He loses his temper and hits her so she falls to the ground. The scene is a complete breakdown of filial piety. In the end, we see the daughter working as a waitress in a bar in Guangzhou. Wearing makeup and dressed in revealing clothes, she walks into the penumbra of urban nightlife, searching for a new life as a worker and consumer rather than through higher education. To most Chinese parents, such a prospect is horrifying, since it is a strong belief that every child has the possibility to have a better life if he or she is willing to work hard enough to stand out from the crowd. However, ensuring this is largely a parent's responsibility.

Tiger Mothers

In recent years educational debates have often played out globally in relation to the ambiguous rise of China, which has emerged as a figure of both allure and anxiety in Europe and the United States. China's new global image has emerged largely as a result of the global financial crisis, the fact that Shanghai students topped the Programme for International Student Assessment (PISA) tests in 2010 and, on a more intimate level, the impact of Chinese American Yale professor Amy Chua's best seller *Battle Hymn of the Tiger Mother* (2011). In her book, Chua describes how she brought up her two overachieving daughters the Chinese way.

Chua decided that besides being straight-A students, her daughters should also become musical talents, and at the age of fourteen the older daughter played her first concert at Carnegie Hall. Throughout the book Chua insists that confidence comes from being good at something, and becoming good requires rote learning and practicing for hours on end, something she refers to as "the virtuous circle." Chua writes provocatively that Western parents praise their children for mediocre results and are afraid of shaking their self-confidence by asking too much of them; consequently, they are "happy to raise losers" (Chua 2011:25).

The book gave rise to highly polarized reactions in the United States and Europe. Some politicians, educators and laypeople felt that the superiority of what could very broadly be termed liberal childrearing practices was challenged. This was also spurred by the fact that in the United States the demographic situation has changed to such an extent that a very large proportion of students at top American universities are of Chinese or Asian descent. Others dismissed Amy Chua's tiger mother approach as being extreme. In Denmark, debates also went in two directions. Whereas many people saw Chua's childrearing techniques as inhuman and fanatical, others argued that it was about time to stop thinking that children were capable of learning everything by themselves and that in order to compete in a global knowledge economy Danes should learn from the Chinese example. In 2010 a group of Danish high school teachers traveled to China, where they visited various Chinese high schools. They came back in shock. They had expected to find students who were disciplined and diligent, but they met students who not only worked twice as hard as Danish students at home, but also seemed to be creative and not afraid to ask questions. "This was what was so shocking," one teacher stated. "How can we compete when Chinese students are beating us on our own terms?"

In setting out to explain why Chinese parents raise "such stereotypically successful children," Amy Chua herself is aware that she is portraying a cultural stereotype of "the Chinese mother." In the introduction she writes, "I'm using the term 'Chinese mother' loosely. I recently met a supersuccessful white guy from Dakota (you've seen him on television), and after comparing notes we decided that his working-class father had definitely been a Chinese mother" (Chua 2011:4). This brings home the way in which the issue of the sacrifices made in order to achieve a better life for the next generation cannot be fully explained in cultural terms. The book also tells a story of migration and social climbing. Amy Chua's own parents were poor Chinese migrants who arrived in the United States in the

1950s, where her father was offered a scholarship to the Massachusetts Institute of Technology and subsequently worked hard as a first-generation immigrant to create a new life. Amy Chua feels grateful to her parents, who taught her to work hard in order to succeed, and the clue to the story of her tiger-mother ambitions is her dread that her daughters will become too spoiled, having been brought up in luxury and with a Jewish father who pampers them. She thus worries that her daughters will suffer from what she calls "family decline." In the book she confesses, "That's one of the reasons that I insisted Sophia and Lulu do classical music. I knew I couldn't artificially make them feel like poor immigrant kids" (Chua 2011:22). Instead she tried to ensure that they worked hard to develop a higher cultural refinement, something she herself had never achieved. For Amy Chua, self-sacrifice *is* self-realization, even though to the liberal reader it is hard to accept that her daughters' well-being often seems neglected.

In the United States and in Europe reactions were divided. While some found Chua's parenting style outrageous and fanatical, others took it as a case in point for arguing that it is about time the West stopped being too self-appreciative and start doing what it takes to compete in a brave new knowledge society. Yet while the West is looking east, the East is looking west, and in the post-Mao era the question of what is to be sacrificed and by whom has become intensely political.

The Boy Who Killed His Mother

In 2001 the case of a student who killed his mother captured great media attention in China. The story became well known and was incorporated into parental guidance books that fall under the rubric of *suzhi jiaoyu* ("education for quality"), as the case was seen as emblematic of outdated parenting practices that inhibited the development of a person's true potential and, by implication, hindered the development of the nation. This was brought home by the fact that Xu Li was in fact a "good student," albeit not an exceptionally high-achieving one, who then committed the unthinkable crime of killing his own mother (Kuan 2008:118). Teresa Kuan points out that interest in the case reflected the fact that whereas the public is usually left in the dark as to the reasons for a student committing a capital crime, in this case Xu Li had spoken about the murder of his mother publicly on television and in print.[2] Xu Li describes his everyday life in his household, where he had no room of his own (Lu 2001:223–224, cited in Kuan 2008:119). He recalled an incident when he came home ten minutes late from a baseball game and she beat him with a belt. His parents had high expectations for his educational achievement, hoping that he would enter Beijing University, Tsinghua University, or at least Zhejiang University, but he says that, given his grades, this was not a realistic possibility. Sometime during the beginning of high school the animosity intensified, and his mother beat him regularly when he got poor test results.

I felt like, I had already grown up so much, yet she was still treating me like a primary student. It was really hard to bear. I felt stifled [*yayi*]. I liked to play soccer, read, watch television, but mother felt that these activities would affect my studies, and always tried to stop me. When classmates at school were discussing current events and television shows, I didn't know anything and there was nothing I could say. I wanted to read the newspaper, but mother would say that college examinations weren't going to test what was in the papers. (Lu 2001:223–224, cited in Kuan 2008:119)

In this way Xu Li described his life as monotonous and unhappy. When asked about the day of the murder, he recalled that he wanted to join his mother, who was watching television, when she cried out angrily: "I'm telling you, if you can't get into university, I won't give you a second opportunity. If you don't test into the top ten on your finals, I'll break your legs. I'm the one who gave birth to you anyway—it doesn't matter if I beat you to death" (Lu 2001:223–224, cited in Kuan 2008:119).

In an outburst of rage, Xu Li hit his mother with a metal hammer. After aimlessly wandering the streets for a couple of hours, he suddenly realized that he should do something to save his mother's life, but when he returned it was too late (Kuan 2008:121).

Whereas Sophocles' classic myth of Oedipus involved patricide, here the mother is the oedipal figure. Furthermore, it is telling that the antagonism was played out in relation to a controversy over educational achievement. Both in parental guidance books and on the national level, this case became emblematic of bad parenting practices and excessive pressure that were believed to be harmful to the psychology of children and young people. Whereas in imperial China killing one's parents was considered the worst possible offense, liable for the severest forms of punishment and torture, here the murder was actually more or less condoned and symbolically came to denote the death of outdated parenting practices that were holding back the nation and potentially preventing China from attaining its rightful place in the world. Would it be too far-fetched to suggest that in a certain sense the Chinese state wishes to carry out its own oedipal project by proxy, urging parents to enable their children to become independent and self-confident while maintaining social control? This brings to mind the iconoclasm of the Cultural Revolution, where the young Red Guards were urged to attack all forms of patriarchal authority in the form of the Four Olds (Old Ideas, Old Culture, Old Customs, and Old Habits), sometimes being made to denounce their own parents, while Chairman Mao remained the father figure par excellence.

At a meeting of the Standing Committee of the Politburo, former president Jiang Zemin even took the case as a point of departure and expressed the view that all responsible parties, from schools to Party organizations, must work to guide the urgent wishes of parents in the right direction.

"We must not confine our youth in rooms and books all day. . . . It isn't that you must attend university in order to become a talent (rencai). . . . Society needs multiple kinds of talents. Three-hundred and sixty occupations, every occupation has an optimus." (Kuan 2008:126)

Li Peng, the chairman of the Standing Committee of the National People's Congress, is listed as first editor of a parental guidance book titled *The Call of Education for Quality* (Kuan 2008:118). Xu Li is portrayed as an independent and talented youth, who exemplifies the exact opposite of the spoiled, dependent single child of the popular imagination, whereas his mother is portrayed as preventing him from developing his full potential. This shows how the state accepts, to some extent, the oedipal killing of the mother in order to let the young generation develop its true potential.

On the Ambiguous Role of Mothers

Mothers play a great role in the socialization of children in all societies. Saint Augustine's cry "Give me other mothers and I will give you another world" suggests that the importance of parent-child relations for social change was not the sole discovery of Freud (de Mause 1974:2). In her work on parenting practices in the city of Kunming, Teresa Kuan observed what she calls "Jekyll and Hyde moments"—that is, moments in which a mother's mood rapidly shifts from sudden rage to calm reflection (Kuan 2011:77). Chinese mothers face tremendous pressure to raise excellent children and are faced with highly contradictory demands since they are responsible for ensuring that their child excels in his or her studies, while also encouraging the child to act for him- or herself rather than under excessive parental duress. Furthermore, she argues that the traditional saying "Stern father and compassionate mother" (*yanfu cimu*) seems to have been reversed in post-Mao China (Kuan 2008:82).

According to Cecilia Milwertz, the tradition of Chinese mothers having a great responsibility in their children's education goes back to the Confucian ideal of the "virtuous wife and good mother" (Milwertz 1997:162–163). This ideal was reintroduced to China by way of Japan in the nineteenth century. In late imperial China, mothers from elite classes played a major role in their children's moral and intellectual development, instructing them in ritual propriety and also introducing them to the world of literacy (Bray 1997). In the Republican era, women were to be "virtuous wives, virtuous mothers" for the sake of the nation. This ideal was attacked during the Cultural Revolution, then reinvented during the post-Mao period. The norms of good mothering in the post-Mao era entailed both participating in the labor market and being responsible for the education of a "perfect only child" (Milwertz 1997:165–166). This also means taking one's child to extracurricular activities and ensuring that he or she develops other creative talents. Kuan puts it this way: "Now fathers are the compassionate ones, while mothers rule sternly, with the tick-tock of a metronome" (2008:84). In the Chinese popular imagination, being a good mother requires self-sacrifice. Harriet Evans has pointed out that the idea of the self-sacrificial mother seems to exist cross-culturally and undoubtedly also corresponds to empirical practice. She also notes that both sons and daughters work to sustain this self-sacrificial ideal (Evans 2008:191). In China the educational system also promotes this ideal, since the image of the suffering mother is held up to schoolchildren, instilling a sense of guilt in them and a desire to "give something back." According to Ann Anagnost, some Chinese women feel so daunted by the responsibility of inculcating quality into their only child that they refuse motherhood and marriage altogether (Anagnost 2004:206). Here, I think it is also important to note that mothers are vulnerable to blame if their child does not excel in his or her studies.

Compliance

When I met Athena in front of the East Gate of Beijing University during the winter of 2005, my immediate impression was that she was very tense despite her forced smile. She spoke good English, but she spoke in a mechanical way with a heavy American accent overlaying her Chinese diction. "Are you American?" she asked me. "Are you from a famous university?" She seemed slightly disappointed to hear that I was from Copenhagen University, which she had never heard of, but went on to tell me that she was glad to have a chance to improve her oral English since she was preparing to take the TOEFL test in order to study abroad. Her appearance was unusual as she wore jewelry and a lot of girlie hairpins, as well as heavy glasses.

Athena led the way to a busy restaurant across the street, and soon after we sat down in the less-crowded section downstairs, each of us with a bowl of noodles, I asked her about her daily life at the university. After a while, she started to cry and switched to Chinese. "My parents always wanted me to get top grades," she said. Since she had been a little girl she had spent most of her time studying diligently, and this included taking extra lessons in English, mathematics, calligraphy, and piano on weekends. "And only one hundred percent correct in tests was good enough," she said. She told me that a few times she had plagiarized other people's work as well as edited her own grades to make them seem better than they were, and her parents had been very proud of her, though she had felt very guilty and sad.

She told me that her parents were both academics from Beijing and that they had taken the college entrance exams after the end of the Cultural Revolution. Both had been educated in the natural sciences, and she emphasized that her grandfather had been a famous biology professor. Contrary to the story of Xu Li, who described his mother as claustrophobically interfering in all aspects of his life, Athena described her relationship to her parents as characterized by physical and emotional distance, and she spoke of her "parents" categorically rather than of her mother and her father as individuals.

Before attending middle school she had been living at a boarding school— "a very good school," she stressed. During weekends most children went home to visit their parents, but she usually stayed at the school because she could not face the pressure of coming home. In the winter it was really cold and sometimes she was all alone, but she preferred this to visiting her parents and disappointing them.

She felt the same way now. Even though her parents lived in Beijing, she rarely visited them because her grades were not "excellent enough." She lacked self-confidence and mentioned the fact that, being from Beijing, she had been admitted to Beijing University with grades that were lower than those of many other students from other parts of the country. She spent most of her time studying for exams in which she had to learn things by heart. Her parents wanted her to do a master's degree at a top university in the United States. She also wanted to go abroad, but for different reasons. Her plan was to obtain good grades so that she could get a scholarship to go abroad to study, because she wanted to be as far away from her parents as possible in order not to feel the pressure she felt they put on her. "They just want me to be more successful so that I can make more money," she said without irony.

I asked her whether her parents wanted her to be happy. She answered, "They don't know that I am not happy. I am very good at putting on a happy face." She said she hid her "true feelings" from other people, including her friends. She had also been in love with a man who seemed to like her and had wanted to get to know her, but she was "confused," she said, and ended up avoiding him; he eventually lost interest in her.

I was at a loss as to what to say to her. I tried to reassure her by saying, "This is your life, and even if you fail an exam there will always be another possibility." But I was unsure of my own words, and my attempts to lift her spirits felt inadequate and awkward. She tried to assure me that she had developed good ways of managing her time and that this was the most important thing for her. Reverting to English, and smiling again, she suggested that she might introduce me to some of her friends who were very good students. She mentioned two pretty girls who were also good at dancing. It was as if she implied that even though she was a failure herself, she could at least refer me to someone more "excellent" than herself. When I tried to contact her again, she never answered.

The existential psychologist R. D. Laing speaks of the way we sometimes comply with external demands by invoking "a false sense of self." Laing's notion of ontological security implies that people need to belong to and engage in a world of others, lest they become "socially dead" (Laing [1960] 1983:98). Accordingly, every human encounter entails ontological risk, though from an existential point of view what is at stake is not so much the integrity of the self as a balance between the world one calls one's own and the world one experiences as not-self or other. In Athena's own words, her parents were always very proud of her—an observation that also recalls Laing's insight that a child's compliance with what he or she sees as a parental expectation usually amounts to "an excess of being 'good,'" of "never being any trouble."

However, Laing points out that compliance is often prompted less by a desire to live up to the other's expectations than by the dread of what might happen if one were to be oneself in actuality (Laing [1960] 1983:98). Lying and taking on different roles become strategies of the compliant self or the compliant person. This came across in Athena's feeling of guilt when she plagiarized other people's work or secretly edited her exam papers. Laing describes a case of a young man, James, who described himself in the following way: "I am a response to what other people say." Similarly, Athena told me that she was "good at putting on a happy face." She seemed to find it difficult to develop close relationships with other people. She made her parents believe that she was getting better results on her exams than was the case. But she could maintain this illusion only by not seeing them, and therefore she wished to live as far away from them as possible. She also avoided the young man who had been friendly toward her, perhaps feeling unworthy of his attention or afraid of having her "true self" revealed.

Although her strategy of compliance may have been an attempt to restore her sense of inner self, it seemed to have the unintended consequence of making her profoundly unhappy and isolated from other people—as when she recalled being alone in the cold and deserted boarding school. She also described to me how she would find spots for working in different libraries and canteens after closing hours, preferring to blend in with the crowd and not to have to talk to the person sitting next to her. There seemed to be no separation between her parents and her own ideals. Apparently she was trying so hard to live up to an image of the perfect daughter and excellent student that she was risking alienation from her real self.

During our conversation, I had the clear impression that Athena was shifting between two selves, unable to fully reconcile them. I think the fact that I was a total stranger, a foreigner in no way connected to her lifeworld, made her momentarily suspend her "happy face." However, this was probably also the reason that she was unwilling to meet me again, since I got the impression that she was in a vicious circle of trying to live up to the role of being a perfect daughter and a model student. Not for nothing had she chosen Athena, the Greek goddess of education, as her English name.

Autonomy and Belonging

Like Athena, Mandy also responded to my notice on the university intranet because she was keen to practice her oral English. Mandy was not a regular student at Tsinghua. In fact she had already graduated with a degree in English from a university in Nanning, in the south of China, bordering Vietnam, but she had come to Beijing in order to take an exam to become a certified translator. She had failed this test twice already, and her father, who owned a company in southern China, was supporting her financially while she was going to classes at Tsinghua and also applying for jobs. She asked me if there was any way she could help me with my research. After some time, I helped her with her English homework and proofread her job applications. And when she realized that I was doing the tedious and time-consuming work of writing up notes and transcribing interviews that were partly in Chinese and partly in English, she offered to help me with this work. She was extremely enthusiastic about being involved in my research, and although she initially declined my offer of remuneration, she eventually accepted payment for her work before I left Beijing. However, she continued to stress that this experience might improve her chances of finding a translation job, and it was much more interesting than learning English from monotonous educational tapes, as she would normally do.

We thus met regularly, and as we gradually got to know each other better, I became aware that her family was suffering terribly because her stepmother had been missing for several weeks and no one had been able to trace her whereabouts. One day, Mandy told me that her missing stepmother, who was a taxi driver, had been found by the police and that she had been murdered. Mandy was profoundly shocked by the incident, but what concerned her most was that her stepmother's death left her father alone with his preschool daughter, Mandy's half sister. Mandy considered going back home, but for reasons that never became quite clear to me she decided to stay in Beijing, apparently having relatively little contact with either of her parents. On one occasion I invited her to my apartment, where she threw herself wholeheartedly into playing with my son, Benjamin, while I cooked dinner. She seemed very grateful to share this space of familial intimacy. Gradually she confided to me the quandaries of her secret life. It turned out that besides studying for the translation test and looking for work, she was very much engaged in trying to find a husband and was very confused, as she had many suitors. An American-Chinese lecturer at Tsinghua kept sending her e-mail messages and SMSs, which both flattered and puzzled her, and she asked me to help her divine "what they meant." However, her parents were not to know that she had boyfriends or was involved in sexual relationships before marriage.[3]

Several students took the view that there was a time for studying and then a time for settling down. In fact, relatively few of the students I interviewed were in a romantic relationship, and many told me that the most important thing was to study and that romantic relationships were too time-consuming. Of course, such views were perhaps also rationalizations that people used when they did not have a girlfriend or boyfriend. Many students did engage in romantic relationships, and tended to struggle quite a bit as to how to divide their time between work and pleasure, duty and play. Sometimes they kept these relationships secret from their parents.

For some time Mandy had been living with a friend in an apartment, but when this friend's boyfriend also moved in with them, Mandy became frustrated by the lack of privacy and eventually accepted her boyfriend's offer to move into his apartment. He was in love with her and wanted to become engaged to her, but she was very confused about their relationship. She was not really in love with him, she said, but he was such a nice person, and she enjoyed his company, and living with him provided her with a space of freedom that she initially enjoyed. At the same time she was overwhelmed by doubt, especially since she eventually got to know his family, who liked her and started treating her as their son's fiancée. Living with him, she also started taking care of the house, cooking, cleaning, and ironing his clothes as a fiancée should, finding that she was afraid to disappoint her "mother-in-law," who was being so nice to her and whose appreciation she enjoyed. However, her parents did not know she had moved in with him. They thought she was still living with her girlfriend, whom she knew from back home. But living in her boyfriend's apartment, Mandy soon started to feel incarcerated. "It is so nice to meet up with you, because I feel so uncomfortable in the apartment," she said, explaining that because of transportation difficulties, her boyfriend did not return before ten o'clock in the evening.

Sometime after my first meeting with Mandy, she started teaching English as a volunteer at a Christian underground church, where she helped elderly people learn to read the Bible in English. A friend of hers had suggested this possibility. When we spent time together in Beijing, she was very curious and mystified about this world of religion that was opening up to her. "I want to believe," she said, and explained that she found people there to be very considerate and peaceful. But having been brought up with Marxism-Leninism in school, she also found it hard to understand how they could believe in Christianity. The pastor of the church urged her to start reading the Bible, and not long after leaving China, I learned from Facebook that Mandy had been baptized.

Mandy seemed very vulnerable. She did not portray any of the choices she made as truly her own. She moved in with her boyfriend because he wanted her to and because she was squeezed out of her friend's apartment by the latter's boyfriend moving in. She started taking care of her boyfriend's house in order to please him and her putative mother-in-law. Pastor Chen wanted her to become baptized, and eventually she did.

Being separated from her parents, she was not set free but confused about how to make a life of her own: where to find a job, whom to date and whom to marry, and which of her girlfriends and teachers she could really trust. It seemed to me that she neither did what her parents wanted her to do—namely, pass the translation test, find a job, and settle down—nor really figure out what she wanted to do herself. Nor did she succeed in getting a job.

I have remained in contact with Mandy for several years now and we have corresponded, though irregularly. In 2008, she moved to South Carolina in the United States, where she became deeply immersed in a Christian community and found faith in God. She is now completing her senior year with a bachelor's degree in accounting and business management at Limestone College and has been happily married to Wu, who is an old classmate of hers from high school back in Liuzhou, China. She explained that he is in his last year of the Ph.D. program in chemistry at the University of South Carolina, and that though she is slightly anxious about her own prospects of finding a job soon after graduation, on the whole things are looking up for them both. In a moving letter, she explained that they started contacting each other four years ago, a year after they had both arrived in the United States, and they got married in 2012. "He is the best gift from God to me. When I look back, I think my journey with God and having faith in Him cannot be more amazing."

James Ferguson has observed that in liberal thought, dependence on others has often figured as the opposite of freedom. He points out, however, that this may be the result of a particularly American worldview. In South Africa young unemployed black men seem to struggle not so much for independence as for what Ferguson calls "declarations of dependence" that suggest that "being someone implied belonging to someone" (Ferguson 2013:228). Ferguson also points out that "for poor South Africans (as for many other people in the contemporary world) the real terror is not dependence but its absence that is really terrifying—the severing of the thread, and the fall into the social void" (Ferguson 2013:232). Mandy's story highlights this tension between autonomy and dependence. For even though she wanted to separate herself from her parents, the isolation she initially experienced in Beijing made her seek out an alternative community to which she could belong. For some time she sought refuge with her transitional boyfriend and his family. She then found a community of "sisters and brothers" in a Beijing house-church and here she became part of a network that opened a path to the United States.

In writing about the intersubjective turn, Michael Jackson notes: "Singular selves are simultaneously part of a commonalty, sole but also several, not only islands but part of the main" (Jackson 1998:6). It seems that Mandy found this alternative space of belonging partly through becoming part of a foreign milieu, but also by falling in love with her high school acquaintance, through which some bonds to her Liuzhou past remained intact.

A Generation Gap

Whereas Xiao Yu's, Athena's, and Mandy's accounts all give the impression of a degree of loneliness and emotional distance from their parents, Helen emphasized her shared intimacy with her mother.

I met Helen, a student of economics, during the first part of my fieldwork, in 2005. She spoke English with a fluency that startled me, and she seemed relaxed and confident. Her father worked at an electronics company, and even though her mother had a part-time job as a secretary, she identified herself as a housewife who, she said, had made raising her daughter "her career." Helen emphasized that her mother had always been extremely loving and caring and had never put any pressure on her. She spoke very little about her father but said that they had a good relationship, even though they mostly talked about topics like "politics and science." Helen spoke of her mother with great affection:

My mother had a very unhappy childhood. She grew up with her grandparents on her father's side, and her grandmother treated her very cruelly because she was a girl. You know, in traditional China only sons were cherished and girls were considered to be a burden. She did a lot of housework, and her brothers were spoilt and got an education. In fact my mother told me that, when she was pregnant, she was hoping that she would have a daughter.

Helen emphasized that her mother had always been very supportive and had let her find her own way in life, as opposed to her cousin, whom she referred to as her "brother," who had always been under so much pressure from his parents. Helen also emphasized that she and her mother had different personalities:

We are very different, my mother and I. In fact I am a workaholic and she is a housewife. She tells me to relax and to take care of my health. She is really different from most Chinese parents, who force their children to study. It is so desperate! To get the highest marks to enter the best middle school, then the best high school and the best university, and to get a good job and earn a lot of money. But my mother has focused more on my happiness. She wants me to do what I am really interested in, and she supports my decisions. Of course she also wants me to do well, but she will always tell me to just do my best. During the college entrance exams, she put so much effort into my entrance exams. My mother actually took half a year of leave from her job just to help me. You know, just to be able to pay more attention to my daily life, to cook delicious food for me and to make me feel comfortable . . . and actually I think she treats me as her career.

I could not help thinking that perhaps her mother was appropriating her daughter's life as a surrogate for her own, but Helen explained that she and her mother were more intimate than was normally the case between parents and children in China. Her parents knew that she had a boyfriend, and they did not interfere with this relationship. Her mother had even written her a letter containing advice on how she could prevent herself from becoming pregnant, demonstrating an openness that Helen admitted was highly unusual between parents and children in China. In most cases there would be a "generation gap," she explained. Like most parents, her mother was a little worried that the relationship would be too time-consuming and affect her studies, but most important of all, "she trusts me." Helen mentioned that she and her boyfriend got lower grades the semester they met each other because they spent so much time together, but during the second semester they found a balance between spending time together and finding time for their studies.

Her boyfriend's parents, on the other hand, had learned about their relationship by chance, and this had been extremely awkward. On one occasion, Helen's boyfriend had been hospitalized with a broken leg, and she had unexpectedly bumped into his father when they were visiting the hospital at the same time. She recalled that it was a very embarrassing and uncomfortable experience, since he had greeted her formally but he had not spoken to her at all.

When I met Helen again in 2007, she had cut her hair short, her face was slimmer and she looked more mature. She said that so much had happened and that she had a lot to tell me. She had graduated and had worked for a time as an accountant at a foreign company in Beijing. However, she found the work tedious and had quit her job and was applying for a Ph.D. in linguistics at a university in England. For the first time in her life, she told me, she felt that she had discovered what she was really interested in. She said that this was also the first time in her life that she had experienced a "generation gap" (*dai gou*) in relation to her parents. She had realized that until that time it had been easy for her parents to support her choices since she had been following the generally accepted path of studying diligently, entering a top university, choosing a "hot" major (economics), and dating a Tsinghua student who had good marriageable conditions (*tiaojian*). Now they failed to understand her decision to quit her good job in order to study linguistics, which they regarded as a more uncertain future, and were sad that she would be leaving China for England.

Helen had been in London as part of an internship before she ended her studies, and while there she had fallen in love with a young British man and had ended the relationship with her former (Chinese) boyfriend. She said that her parents found it hard to come to terms with the fact that she was seeing a foreigner. She said that they shared the racist idea, typical of their generation, that Chinese and foreigners belonged to different races and should not mix, since their children would become anomalous: neither one thing nor another. She said that they did not put any direct pressure on her to change her mind, but she felt that communication with her mother had become more formal and awkward, and this made her sad. When she spoke to her mother on the phone she found that they would often talk about trivial things in order to avoid hurting each other. In this way, although Helen had never experienced parental pressure and explained that her parents had always supported her decisions, it became clear to her that "a generation gap" had arisen after she had been abroad, since her parents were uncomfortable with and worried about the choices she had made. In this sense she clearly separated herself from the will of her parents, and the result was a strong feeling of melancholia associated with separating from the world of her parents and her primary bonds.

Traveling in Time

For Sun Li, too, losses and gains were inextricably connected. As she received her graduation certificate in the summer of 2007 from the Institute of Environmental Science and Engineering at Tsinghua, her face gleamed with pride under the characteristic black graduation cap. She was one of many students who, one by one, received their graduation certificates on the stage and shook hands with the director of the department in front of their parents, grandparents, and other family members in the large, crowded auditorium. A few weeks earlier, Su Li had received an admission letter from a university in the United States to do a Ph.D. in environmental science.

Sun Li was the only student of her grade with a rural background. Her parents were farmers in Jiangsu province, but they were unable to attend her graduation, because they could not afford two train tickets to Beijing. They had never visited the capital, and in many ways Sun Li and her parents had become worlds apart. Most students from China's poorer rural areas viewed obtaining a Beijing residence permit (*hukou*) and a well-paid job in the capital as the height of their expectations for a bright future, whereas students from better-off urban backgrounds often dreamed of going abroad. However, for Sun Li higher education had provided a trajectory of social mobility that might ordinarily have taken several generations, and this was in a sense tantamount to traveling in time. Far from her parents' lives of tilling the fields and part-time wage labor in the nearest village, she envisioned her own future as part of a global, highly educated elite. She imagined herself dedicated to solving problems related to global climate change, addressing issues she considered vital, given the pollution of rivers in her hometown.

Sun Li told me that she had always liked to study. "In fact, before I came to Beijing, I always felt that studying was the most interesting thing in life, because there is nothing else to do in my hometown," she said. She explained that when she visited her parents, she preferred to stay indoors reading much of the time, and people found this behavior strange and even abnormal. Her mother would constantly urge her to come outside, to mix with other villagers and be introduced to young men, but she dreaded this and found ways to escape.

"In some ways, when I go back home I experience a lot of pressure," she said. In her case, parental pressure had nothing to do with obtaining high grades. "My parents want me to get married and have a child. It is all they think of. They are building a house for me close to theirs! They won't listen to me when I urge them to stop this project!" She said that they were proud that she had made it into a top university in China, but they felt that, given her age, it was about time she started thinking about getting married and setting up a family of her own. They were eager that she should give birth to a son and thus continue the family line. Being twenty-two years old, she was the only one among her former high school classmates who had not yet married and had a baby. They did not approve of her idea of going to the United States for a five-year doctoral program. She explained:

They don't know much about the world outside China. Some of their neighbors tell them negative stories about life "abroad"—that education in America is of low quality and that when young people go abroad they forget about their responsibilities [toward their kin and their country]. They are jealous because in some cases they cannot even pay for their children's high school education. But when people start talking like this, my parents defend me. Although they can never agree with me, they love me and they want me to be happy.

In other words, despite her parents' skepticism, it appears that they let her do what she wanted out of love, and perhaps also because they had no other choice. When I asked her what they were going to do with the house they were building, she exclaimed, "I don't know!" But she went on to say that perhaps it would be a good investment and that they would also really like to move to Beijing to live with her during their old age. But she also considered this scenario unrealistic. "They are not accustomed to urban life," she said. "But like most Chinese farmers they automatically think that urban life is better."

Sun Li had a part-time job as an English teacher at a middle school in Beijing and used the money she earned for activities like going to the theater, concerts, plays, museums, and exhibitions. She had not told her parents about this job, since it would have been hard for them to understand how she spent her money, such as spending forty yuan on a theater ticket. So this part-time job gave her some independence to explore the city and find out that "life has so much more to offer than only studying!"

Having moved from the Chinese countryside to an elite university in the capital, and being confronted with the prospect of going to the United States to study for a Ph.D., she had in a sense undertaken what Marianne Gullestad has called a "class journey" (Gullestad 2002:73). In existential terms, she had reversed the relationship between parents and children and won a great degree of independence. At the same time, she tended to regret that she and her parents no longer shared the same lifeworld. This melancholia is partly an inescapable aspect of growing up, since it also entails a potentially painful separation. In Sun Li's case this separation was exacerbated by higher education, which caused her to live in a lifeworld that was different from that of her parents, though it may be more to the point to say that her possibilities for belonging in either world were compromised.

Going Abroad and Returning

For Sun Li, education was more than a means to an end. It was an end in itself and a source of fulfillment. Unmistakably ambitious, Liu Xing felt the same way. Liu Xing and I met regularly for coffee, and we shared a common interest in literature and films. She stood out as a somewhat taciturn, yet acutely intelligent, thoughtful, and very considerate law student at Tsinghua University, and she hailed from the city of Harbin in Heilongjiang province in the north of China. She always asked me how my research was going and whether she could help me in any way. Her English was fluent, and she made me self-conscious about my Chinese. When Liu Xing was accepted into Tsinghua University, a local newspaper in Harbin featured an article about her mother, a successful career woman, who had brought up her daughter in accordance with the norms of *suzhi jioayu*. In the interview, Liu Xing's mother stressed that she had always let Liu Xing find her own interest in studying, but that she had supported her daughter's interest in pursuing knowledge that was not directly related to the school curriculum by buying foreign as well as Chinese novels for her, as well as history books, since this was what she was interested in. Liu Xing had always been a diligent student, but her mother had stressed that she should also get out of the house and develop her creative interests in music and art.

Liu Xing's parents were both white-collar workers at a state-owned company in Harbin. They both had university degrees. Liu Xing would have liked to study sociology, but she had chosen to study law, which she was also interested in and which at the same time promised better career opportunities. However, unlike her parents, whom she found to be naive in this regard, she was very critical of the Chinese judicial system, and this, she said, was the main reason she wanted to study for a Ph.D. in the United States.

One day I had lunch with Liu Xing and her boyfriend, Zhou, who was also a Tsinghua law graduate. He was employed at a private company, and he responded somewhat ironically to her claim that it was her own choice to do a Ph.D. "It is no secret that your mother really wants you to become a doctor," he said, with a twinkle in his eye. Liu Xing blushed, gave him an annoyed look, and insisted that it was most certainly her own decision to pursue doctoral study. Even though Liu Xing and her parents had more or less the same desires and aspirations for her future, she experienced a sense of self-determination, or a balance between her mother's aspirations and her own.

I have remained in contact with Liu Xing over the years and have followed her life at a distance, knowing that she completed her Ph.D. in law in Indiana. When I returned to Beijing in 2012 for a stint of fieldwork, she had recently returned to Beijing as well, after five years in the United States. We met in a coffee shop in the San Li Tun Village. We had a view of the little street that led to the school I had attended when I lived in Beijing in the 1980s, around the time when she was born. I told her that this had been the road to my school and that this area used to be a traditional *hutong* neighborhood, with small, winding roads that contained markets with small vendors selling live chickens, meat, and vegetables. Sometimes I would get lost with my bike in the crowded little alleys. She marveled at the thought that I had actually been in this place before she had been born.

"I read your dissertation," she confessed. I had sent it to her as promised, but did not know until that moment if she had read it and what she thought of the way in which I had portrayed her. "Most of it seems pretty accurate," she said with a shy smile. "It was interesting to read about what I was like then. I think I have changed quite a lot." She told me about how her relationship with her former boyfriend had gradually come to an end and how he was now married to a very successful woman from an extremely wealthy family. She had since been in another relationship, but it had also ended.

Liu Xing said that she had very much liked having her own life in the United States, living by herself, with her cat, whom she adored, and that she had struggled to stay both secluded in a Chinese community and involved in American life. Most of all, she had been extremely busy with her studies, as well as working as an intern in a law firm, and in a sense she had had little time to think about where she was going and what she wanted to do. She was faced with these big questions now, she said. "I expected it to be difficult to move to another country, but this was actually easier than I thought. There are so many Chinese students in the U.S., so I could in fact feel at ease there. However, I had not expected returning to Beijing to be difficult."

"Why did you come back to China?" I asked her.

"Because of my parents," she said. "All of a sudden I missed them and think I have to be closer to them."

Liu Xin went on to talk about how she felt caught between two lives. She had never really adjusted to life in the United States. "I liked my life a lot, but I could never become truly American," she said. At the same time, she said, she now felt somewhat estranged from Beijing, as if she was an outsider watching life from a distance. "So much has changed while I was away." She talked about how unemployment had skyrocketed. Or perhaps, she reflected, she had simply never been aware that it existed, since she had lived her life inside the small world of the Tsinghua campus. Her parents had just bought her an apartment, and although she was thrilled about moving into her own flat, real estate prices had soared, and she realized and regretted how much she still depended on her parents. "When will I ever grow up?" she asked, adding that she had recently been looking for a place to rent, checking out all options, and had been appalled to realize that sometimes college graduates lived together in small spaces, several people sharing a flat, and that these flats were sometimes located in basements that did not see the light of day and with contracts that did not seem fully legal to her. She was aware that she was fortunate. She felt confident that she would quite easily find a job in a law firm in Beijing, but the question was how time-consuming and fulfilling the work would be. She was also happy to be close to her parents again and they were overjoyed to have her back. However, she felt that she herself had changed and she did not quite feel at home in Beijing. Part of her was still in the Midwest, she explained. She was finding it hard to get used to the crowds of Beijing and the way everybody seemed to be constantly struggling to get ahead.

In a sense, "paradise had been redefined." Vanessa Fong uses this phrase to capture the ambiguity experienced by many Chinese transnational students who go abroad for further education, expecting life outside of China to be a paradise (*tiantang*), only to end up defining China as a paradise that they have lost during their time abroad. Sometimes they feel caught between Chinese and American utopias. One young woman who spent ten years studying and working in Japan, put it this way after returning to China: "Sometimes I think I want to go abroad again, to Japan or another country, if I see an opportunity. But sometimes I think that's foolish. There are many things I'm not used to in China anymore, having been abroad for 10 years. But there are also many things I'll never be used to abroad. I'm not used to anywhere anymore" (Fong 2011:220).

Perspectives

By invoking the notion of the oedipal project in this chapter, I have wanted to highlight both what is universal about relationships between parents and children and the significant differences that exist across human societies and between people living within the same society. In all societies, a child is able to grow up and become an independent person only through some sort of separation from the will of the parents. In China, though young people's relationships to their parents are radically different depending on social situation, upbringing, gender, field of study, previous experiences, and so on, being an only child seems to intensify oedipal tensions because a generation of only children faces the prospect of taking care of both parents.

When my interlocutors invoke the concept of "generation gap" (*dai gou*), this rarely involves *direct* conflicts in which two opposing wills cannot be reconciled. There is an existential element underlying the notion of a generation gap, which can be understood as a form of oedipal tension, and which can be construed as a "blocked oedipal project." Many of the students I have studied follow and try to live up to their parents' aspirations for them, because they feel obliged to reciprocate the sacrifices their parents have made for them in terms of having given them the gift of life, as well as having enabled them to receive an education. Rather than directly opposing the will of their parents, students often say that they do not want to hurt their parents' feelings, and instead resort to secret lives, such as having girlfriends or boyfriends their parents do not know about. But this secrecy can create estrangement between the student and his or her parents. As a result, the young person may feel restrained from growing up and coming into his or her own.

Depending on their social backgrounds or their different starting points in life, it seems that my interlocutors face quite different existential dilemmas in relation to their parents. In contrast to students from urban areas, students who come from rural areas have usually grown up with siblings. They do not experience the same pressure of being the "only hope" of their parents, and they clearly experience a lesser degree of parental pressure to excel in their studies. Furthermore, having come a long way from their natal homes and having had to manage on their own in the totally different urban setting usually has fostered some sense of reflection. Even though they sometimes find it very difficult to compete with students who have been brought up in an urban and more intellectual environment, they seem to experience a greater sense of governing their own destiny.

However, students' expectations that they should ultimately reverse the generational contract in the sense of repaying their parents' sacrifices by taking care of them during their old age weigh heavily on them. Most often the thought of returning to their hometown to set up a family there and to care for their parents is strongly at odds with the kind of urban/cosmopolitan future they imagine for themselves. Bringing their parents to live with them in Beijing is also, in many cases, an impossible endeavor for most young people, since living costs in Beijing are too high, and they have an acute sense that their parents will not be able to adapt to the urban environment. Moreover, the parents would feel isolated and estranged in a foreign world, rather like migrants who cannot speak with the right diction or understand local norms of comportment.

Gender differences also give rise to different existential tensions between parents and children. The oedipal tension played out in several of the young women's relationships with their parents was related to their sexual maturity and the question of whom to date and whom to marry. To Sun Li, parental pressure was the pressure to have a child rather than to excel in education or a future career. Helen's parents disapproved of her foreign boyfriend. The issue of premarital relationships was in part what drove Mandy to lead a secret life, disconnecting her from her parents and, oddly, making her fall into the gendered role of being her boyfriend's housekeeper and a respectable "daughter-in-law" as she struggled to pass the translation exam and to get a job in Beijing.

Just as the movement from rural to urban China creates certain tensions, so does the crossing of the boundary between China and the wider world. Helen previously recalled that her mother had supported her decisions, and she did not find it problematic that her mother regarded the upbringing of her daughter as "her career" until a conflict of interest arose. After Helen returned from London, she and her mother had different views about how Helen's life should unfold. The strong sense of connectedness she experienced in relation to her mother eventually took on the form of an oedipal conflict, which was overcome by Helen's choosing her own way in life, but with the result that a form of polite conviviality replaced the previous sense of trust and intimacy that she and her mother had shared.

These oedipal dilemmas echo the migrant's struggle to change his or her identity in relation to changing situations (Jackson 2013:206). Whereas R. D. Laing emphasizes the potentially pathological aspect of a "divided self," Philip Bromberg makes a somewhat different observation. Even when humans are faced with seemingly irreconcilable imperatives or desires, they do not fall apart. Indeed, a "multiple self" is not necessarily incompatible with normal mental functioning, because "a person can access simultaneously a range of self-states that, despite their contrasting and even opposing perspectives on personal reality, are able to engage in internal dialogue" (Bromberg 1993:186, cited in Jackson 2013:206). Perhaps it is only when this internal dialogue is lost that we can talk of a schizophrenic self. So while the migrant's ability to shift between different self-states and seemingly incompatible experiences does not imply an inability to function normally, it may, as was the case for Jing Jing, lead to loneliness, despair, and regret.

Steven Mitchell points out that the view of the self as multiple and discontinuous "is grounded in a temporal rather than a spatial metaphor: selves are what people do and experience over time rather than something that exists someplace" (Mitchell 1995:101). Here it may be important to point out that while it is also true that the idea of a static self is possibly an undesirable illusion, a multiplicity of self-states can be painful and sometimes unbearable. Not all double binds can be resolved. These *aporias* are part of the human condition, and as we go through our lives our perspectives on them inevitably change. However, the passage to modernity or the transition from rural to urban China and to a global village, such as the one Sun Li experienced, seems to be inevitably accompanied by grief and guilt. There are always strings attached, and the new life gained may be shadowed by the loss of the old one.

As I am writing (September 2013), China has just revised the Protection of the Rights and Interests of Elderly People law, and a clause now stipulates: "Family members living apart from the elderly should frequently visit or send greetings to elderly persons."[4] However, no sanctions go with this change of law, and one can only wonder whether such an attempt to address a moral problem will lead to societal change or instill a greater sense of guilt in those who feel unable to meet this responsibility. While my interlocutors see filial piety as an important virtue, they regard the law as a joke. However, it is interesting to note that they do not seem to regard the provision of care to elderly people as a responsibility of the state.

Chapter 3

Youth and the Party-State

JUST AFTER STARTING MY FIELDWORK, I remember browsing through the newest issue of the *Lonely Planet* guide to Beijing at the multi-storied bookstore on Beijing's famous shopping street, Wang Fu Jing. In the historical section of the book there was a whited-out section. However, by holding the page up to the sunlight it was still possible to read what had been meticulously erased by hand using whiteout—namely, a description of the army's attack on students and protesters during the Tiananmen incident of 1989. During my fieldwork the topic was rarely brought up. Since the students of Beijing University in particular were among the main organizers of the protests, I could not help wondering whether the Chinese government's attempt at censorship had been so successful that the students were in fact ignorant of the incident, whether they accepted the public silencing, thinking it best to let sleeping dogs lie, or whether they regarded it as a historical incident that was simply irrelevant to their generation.

As Ghassan Hage has noted (1996a:472–477), the family evokes images of both maternal care and patriarchal control, an ambiguity that is carried over into images of the state.[1] From a phenomenological point of view, this involves exploring the state as both an actual and an imagined entity. With the disappearance of the *danwei* system and the social security provided by socialism, it has been argued that "the state is ending the paternalism that was the hallmark of the socialist era" (Woronov 2007:30). The road to national development is now pursued through self-development. However, in focusing on how the state is experienced, remnants of the idea of a paternal/maternal state are clearly still present in young people's imagination.

In the Chinese educational system, love of country and love of the party are taught together. Chinese students are repeatedly taught about the national humiliations China faced before the 1949 revolution and how the Communist Party ended them. University students must take courses every year in basic

Communist philosophy, including Marxism, and the thought of Mao Zedong and Deng Xiaoping. Even though most young Chinese people express a strong sense of nationalism, it seems that few students, not to mention their teachers, really take these courses seriously. Many students regard it as "a joke" or a waste of time and say that they show up because there is a roll call, only to spend their time sleeping, chatting, or studying for other courses. The paper they have to submit at the end of the term is quite easy to write, and many students readily admit that they plagiarize one another's essays.

We have seen how some students remember, in particular, their mother's discipline, or *guan*, as a form of care and control. But can the Chinese state continue to succeed in casting itself as a caring master, exercising "control as care?"[2] And how do university students experience state attempts at making paternal/maternal love into political instruments for the creation of a harmonious society?

According to Yunxiang Yan, it was at the turn of the twentieth century that the word "youth" (*qingnian*) acquired a social meaning, and he shows how the formation of a youth culture was tied closely to the policies of the party-state. Before then, no intermediary stage was recognized between childhood and adulthood, and a child was not considered to be a full person (Yan 1999:75). A person remained an unreliable, immature child until marriage, and one would be stigmatized if one remained in this position for too long. The expression "young and ignorant" (*nianyou wuzhi*) was used both as a rationale for not taking youngsters seriously and as an explanation for their wrongdoings. A new stage in the life course, "the youth period" (*qingnian*) was in fact created during the Mao era. After 1949, the Communist Party and the state continued to mobilize young people in both rural and urban areas.[3] The Red Guards constituted the most radical attack on parental authority, abusing and assaulting teachers and even kin. Despite this very violent repudiation of patriarchal authority, Chairman Mao remained an almost deified father figure.

Even though the Communist Party played a crucial role in the creation of "youth" as a social category, unintended consequences followed. With the emergence of youth as a category in its own right, a particular youth culture also emerged. This gave rise to three consequences in particular, which may not have been anticipated by the Communist Party leaders, namely, anti-authority tendencies, a lack of respect for corrupt party members, and an awareness of individual rights (Yan 1999:87–90). In this way, the generational gap Yan identified in the countryside can be understood as a gap between rural and urban aspirations and also, to a large extent, as a gap between ideals and reality. "Although the collective preferences of the young vary depending on the changes in the larger social setting, from reciting quotations from Mao's work to wearing printed T-shirts to tastes in pop-music, the end result is the same: youngsters now constitute a distinct group" (Yan 1999:87–90). Accordingly, young people in rural areas now openly oppose their elders and refuse to be told what to do.

Since the reform era, the creation of a highly educated Chinese elite has been seen as a vital condition for improving China's economy and enabling China to pave its way into the first world (Fong 2004). However, the state has unknowingly created a potential Frankenstein monster, which must be held in check lest it threaten the patriarchal authority of the party-state. Yet I find it striking that the anti-authoritarian tendencies of the rural youth described by Yan seldom correspond to my impression of urban elite students, who only rarely directly challenge parental or government authority. To some extent schools contain the monster, and teachers mediate between parents and state, playing the roles of both quasi family member and the state's moral agent.

On the Ambiguous Role of Teachers

At Tsinghua University and Beijing University, I noticed that professors addressed their former teachers as *laoshi*, and students of the same teacher often referred to each other as "siblings," calling each other *shige, shidi, shijie*, or *shimei*.[4] My interlocutors also gave me to understand that when someone has been your teacher, you must continue to address him or her as such for the rest of your life. Andrew Kipnis has pointed out that in China the term "teacher" (*laoshi*) is in many ways like a kinship term (2009:216–218). The saying *weiren shibiao* is on display in many schools throughout the country and can be translated as "act as a person of exemplary virtue" or "be worthy of the appellation teacher." This saying poignantly captures some of the tension between the teacher's roles as a quasi family member and as an extension of the state.[5] To some extent teachers embody the state, but at the same time they act in loco parentis, though individual teachers play this role in their own manner.

The teachers I interviewed and spent time with during my fieldwork, especially the female teachers, emphasized a feeling of moral obligation not only to teach their students the curriculum so that they could do well, but also to take *care* of their students if they encountered any kind of trouble. This included making sure that they took their studies seriously and did not jeopardize their future. At the same time, however, most teachers seemed to feel inadequate in this regard, since there was very little close interaction between teachers and students. One teacher put it this way: "The students perhaps feel that they know me, but I don't know them." Because of the large class sizes, it was difficult for teachers to really get to know the students' perspectives. In addition, the pressures of work and of family life took up their time.

My impression was that students experienced little interaction with their teachers, although teachers sometimes became strong role models, in some sense replacing parents as significant figures of authority. This was certainly the case for Jia Ling.

Jia Ling

When I met Jia Ling one day in front of Tsinghua University's biggest canteen (the *Wan ren shi tang*, literally "ten thousand people's dining hall"), she looked radiant in her new red jacket. She seemed to be in a very good mood, and she told me that she had been given a prize for her teaching skills. As a result of a students' poll, she had been voted as one of the most popular teachers. She was very proud of this formal recognition, which also included a small financial bonus. Though the bonus was symbolic, it actually made a difference in her case because she was providing for her mother financially. It came across clearly in my interviews with her students that Jia Ling was a role model for several of the girls, including Liu Xing and Helen, whom I got to know quite well and whose stories I presented in Chapter 2. Their aspirations to go abroad for further study and their critical views of the party mirrored Jia Ling's own views closely.

Jia Ling was not a typical teacher. She was in her mid-thirties and thus younger than her students' parents and in fact closer to the students in age. In Jia Ling's own experience, she said, she often felt a "generation gap" in relation to older teachers, who were about the age of her parents and therefore belonged to a generation that had been "damaged by the Cultural Revolution." As a result, she felt that "they tend to boss people around." Her students commented to me that she was remarkable in the sense that she told them things about her own life and also seemed interested in getting to know their perspectives.

Helen said that she admired Jia Ling so much because "she knows what she really wants do in life and she does not just follow the trend." Helen was referring to the fact that Jia Ling was not married, although she was over the normal marriageable age, and so she came across as very independent, resisting family and social pressures. Furthermore, Jia Ling was applying to do a Ph.D. in England, to study Chinese literature from "a foreign perspective." Helen found this idea very original, since while she was interested in broadening her mind and learning from life abroad, she remained attached to her cultural roots. In pursuing this dream, Jia Ling was "choosing her own way," since her parents disapproved of her plans to go abroad. Both Helen's and Jia Ling's parents found Tsinghua to be the ultimate symbol of success and did not think England had anything that China could not offer.

Jia Ling was the youngest in a family of five sisters. "My parents really tried hard to have a boy," she told me with a smile. Her life course had evolved very differently from those of her four sisters, since she was the only one among them who had a university degree. She was also the only one who was unmarried and childless. Her sisters all worked at the same factory in Zhejiang province, where both her parents had also worked. She quite often spoke with deep regret of the sister who was closest to her in age, whom she described as very bright but "too sensitive." When she had to take the college entrance exams she panicked and received a very low result, which was a shock to everybody because she had been at the top of her class. Jia Ling's sister was now extremely afraid that her own children would repeat what she saw as the worst mistake of her life. Jia Ling, on the other hand, felt that her sisters put too much pressure on their children. Whenever she came home to visit her family, her sisters always said that it was such a shame that she did not have any children of her own. They thought she would be such a "good mother" because she would be able to give her children so much due to her high level of education and her teaching position at Tsinghua University in Beijing.

When Jia Ling visited her sisters, they always wanted her to teach their children English, but she insisted that it was more important for the children to spend time playing. They needed time to relax, to be idle and to enjoy life. Her sisters felt that since she was not a mother herself, she could not fully understand the pressures they faced. Furthermore, they argued, "How do you expect us to take this view seriously when you have always had your own nose poked into a book?" Her sisters felt that Jia Ling had come so far in life *because* she had always been a good student and that she had made it into university *because* she had done well on her college entrance exams. Jia Ling considered herself extremely lucky, but she felt guilty in relation to her sisters, who she considered had been less lucky than she. When Jia Ling was an undergraduate at Zhejiang University, an English couple who were guest professors and had no children of their own had helped her get a scholarship to Manchester University. In this way Jia Ling had obtained a master's degree abroad. She stayed in her mentors' house for two years, and they had even given her a small allowance, enabling her to live without financial support from her family. With a degree from abroad, she had been able to find a prestigious job as an English teacher at Tsinghua University.[6]

Jia Ling taught a small group of graduate students oral English, and she told her students about her family background as a way of setting the scene for discussing family relationships, marriage, and life plans. Jia Ling had also shared her skepticism about the Communist Party with her students. She had told them how at one point she had considered joining the party, since it might be possible to make real social changes only by working from *within* it. But she had changed her mind, feeling that it would be a case, as she put it, of "the party changing me, not me changing the party."

Filial Piety and Nationalism

According to Liu Xing, her parents were party members and would have liked her to join the party. Although they never put any pressure on her to do so, they felt that as a lawyer this would have been a wise strategy, since this might guarantee her a career as a civil servant. Liu Xing was nevertheless skeptical of the party, even though at one point she thought that the only way to work toward improving the Chinese society was to work from within the party. But she was not willing to "become the party," since it would probably be impossible to make any real changes. This argument was practically identical to Jia Ling's view, which was understandable, given that Jia Ling was Liu Xing's teacher and in a sense came to replace her parents as a figure of authority. However, in this case, it did not mean identifying with the state as a father figure. Liu Xing said of the party members at the university: "They take themselves so seriously, talking nonsense and telling other people what to do and how to think. In my view they are ridiculous!"

Even though her parents urged her to join the party for pragmatic and strategic reasons, Liu Xing felt that there were other roads to take, such as going to the United States to do a Ph.D. in law. She was convinced that the American educational system was much more "advanced," to use her own word, in the sense that there was room for critical thinking. However, she stressed that she wanted to return to China after obtaining her degree. "I will always remain Chinese," she said. She did not want her children to become "bananas," she said, a euphemism for overseas Chinese, who look Chinese (yellow), but are really foreign (white) inside.

Liu Xing said that she was unable to relate to the overseas Chinese students at Tsinghua, whose Chinese was so poor that she could not understand how they could communicate with their own parents. She also found them to have less self-discipline than most regular Chinese students, to be spoiled and to spend money lavishly. She wanted her child or children to grow up in China and to remain Chinese. Her thoughts therefore resonated with Vanessa Fong's work, which draws attention to the fact that a generation gap between parents and children does not preclude filiality (Fong 2004; also Kipnis 2009:215). Furthermore, Fong refers to Michael Herzfeld's notion of "cultural intimacy" in order to make a connection between the ways in which young people see their relationship to their nation *and* their relationship with their parents as equally "filial":

Well educated and raised on wealthier societies' images and brand names, they felt that they did not resemble the "backwardness" they associated with their motherland any more than they resembled their long-suffering, poorly educated parents. Yet teenagers shared with their elders a powerful sense of nationalism based on the belief that they could no more cease to be "people of China" than they could cease to be their parents' children. When teenagers in Dalian saw the Chinese nation, they were looking at their parents; when they expressed devotion to their nation, they recalled their devotion to their parents, with the uneasy combination of love, ambivalence, frustration and duty that such filial devotion entailed (Fong 2004:644–645).

Liu Xing's ambiguous relationships with her parents and her country fit well into this description of filial obligation as nationalism. Fong's discussion, however, avoids the issue of party membership. The generation gap that Liu Xing experienced in relation to her parents had less to do with different attitudes toward brand names and consumption patterns than with the ambiguity she experienced in relation to her parents' devotion to the party. Her parents' outdated attitude toward the party appeared to embarrass her, although she never expressed this directly and always expressed great affection for her parents, who had always let her choose her own way in life. Liu Xing maintained that for her the party was largely irrelevant. She described it as a fossil standing in the way of progress toward the more democratic society she hoped China would become in the future. However, she was emotionally bound to her country in the same way that she was bound to her parents, and was quite vehement in declaring, "I don't have to be a member of the party to love my country."

The Blocking of Water Wood

Early one morning in 2005, a group of some thirty students as well as a few teachers gathered near the semi-frozen lakes in the western part of the Tsinghua campus to carry out a silent protest against the closing of the university's intranet, "Water Wood" (Shui Mu). This was the result of a decree coming straight from the minister of education. Nobody held up any banners, and no protests were shouted. It was an entirely peaceful and quiet gathering, with students standing together sipping tea from their thermoses. But the spirits of the group were low.

Liu Xing was among the protesters, and she was very upset by the shutting down of the intranet. Like many students, she spent a lot of time on the university intranet, which provided various forms of practical information regarding courses and extracurricular activities. It was also a forum in which students discussed various topics among themselves, as well as with former students, including those who were now studying or living and working abroad. The intranet had been blocked so that non-students, people who no longer lived on campus, could not log on and participate in the chat rooms. About one year earlier, the intranet of Beijing University, known as "Hurly Burly" (Yita Yutu), had also been blocked because students were debating human rights and other politically sensitive issues. Beijing University had a history of rebellion, and the Chinese leadership was particularly keen to ensure that no kind of disturbance should happen there again. I was told that every year on June 4, the anniversary of the 1989 Tiananmen protests, secret police patrolled the campus to ensure that nothing took place that might stir things up.

However, it seems that the closing of Shui Mu came as a surprise to Tsinghua students. They often saw Beijing University as a potentially rebellious place, but they were surprised that a similar ban would take place at their university. Tsinghua University was generally seen as being more conservative, pragmatic and apolitical, devoted to solving real problems in the world, as opposed to being carried away by abstract ideals and busily "talking as if they were leaders."

The idea that the Internet would necessarily have a democratizing effect on China is something often repeated in the Western media, but this is, I think, a form of wishful thinking. The Internet is not necessarily a force that will be used to bring about political reform, and it could just as well be used to further nationalist causes as democratic ones. Nevertheless, in the case of the Tsinghua University intranet, the issue of censorship was in fact a main concern, the principal reason it had been closed to outsiders wishing to log on. This action left students feeling disappointed, angry, and bewildered. Nobody knew exactly what had happened, though everybody seemed to agree that somebody must have crossed the line in terms of what it was acceptable to chat about.

This view of the state as a parent figure[7] was also echoed in Wu Liang's response to the closing of Water Wood. During a taped interview with me, Wu Liang said that he found its closing to be "just OK," because as a party member it was his duty to serve society and to make sacrifices for his country. His use of the term "sacrifices" is striking.

Even though the Communist Revolution rejected Confucianism, viewing it as a feudal tradition that hindered national progress, sacrifice to gods and ancestors was, according to Stephen Feuchtwang, transposed in party slogans to sacrifice for the sake of the Greater Us (*da wo*) or the common good of the nation or "people" (Feuchtwang 2002:207). Class solidarity replaced family loyalty, while the ethos of family loyalty through filial piety was replaced by the need to bear sacrifices for the people/nation. In other words, even though the Communist Revolution and the period of Maoism attempted to eradicate Confucian norms that were seen to be reactionary and sought to replace family loyalty with loyalty to the state, a new social imaginary of sacrifice was invented.

The story of Lei Feng, the socialist hero who tirelessly served the people, is paradigmatic in conveying the Maoist ethos of working selflessly for the nation (Farquhar 2002:37). Lei Feng was a model soldier who died in a truck accident in 1962. After his death, his story was elaborated as an example for others. During the Cultural Revolution, city youth volunteered for immersion in the countryside to show their devotion to Maoist socialism, and they competed with one another for hard work in the fields and to be seen as "paragons of selflessness" (Feuchtwang 2002:204).

At one point, Wu Liang glanced suspiciously at my tape recorder, and I responded by immediately turning it off. He then continued in a slightly different vein, saying, "It is as if we are children . . . why shouldn't the government have faith in Tsinghua students' ability to be responsible?" Wu Liang's response was reminiscent of a child who is hurt and disappointed that his parents show such little faith in him. Addressing the closing of the intranet of Beijing University, he pointed out that "the students of Beida have a tradition of being irresponsible, rebellious, wanting to cause trouble." But he felt that Tsinghua students were "responsible," and that there ought to be no need to subject them to *unnecessary* control.

The blocking of Tsinghua's intranet, following the blocking of Beijing University's intranet a year earlier, made students reflect on the role of the state. Even though most students used the intranet for apolitical reasons, the knowledge that it had been shut off from outsiders, as well as overseas Chinese and former graduates of the university, made them feel that they were being subjected to political control. Wu Liang did not seem to question the fact that the state sought to control its citizens. Rather, he was disappointed that the government should exercise "*unnecessary*" control over Tsinghua students, whom he felt to be "responsible," unlike students of Beijing University who might threaten social harmony by creating chaos (*luan*). Whether or not the students were party members, whether they were politically engaged or not, they experienced the events as blocking their freedom to express their ideas and to communicate with people outside China. Toward the end of my fieldwork, I heard from some students at Beijing University that their intranet had reemerged. It was still called Yita Yutu, but the characters used were different from the former ones. In this way they had creatively come up with a way of bypassing state censorship.

1989

Earlier, I described Helen, who experienced a "generation gap" in relation to her parents after she had been abroad because her parents disapproved of her British boyfriend. Helen also told me that her experience of being abroad had made her aware of political issues that she had previously known nothing about. Her English boyfriend had sent her illegal videos about human rights issues and video clips of the Chinese army's attack on protesters in 1989, and for the first time in her life she was afraid of what could happen. "What if somebody catches me and puts me in jail?" she said. Then she awkwardly dismissed this thought as ridiculous and paranoid. Yet she had not been able to stop thinking about this issue, she said. Her parents had never told her about this incident, though when she asked them about it, they remembered it very well.

Hu, a physics student at Beijing University from a small town in Jiangxi province, also passionately broached this subject. Both of his parents were party members, and his father had a government position. Hu said that his parents urged him not to become a member, but rather to stay out of politics and instead to focus on his studies and pursue a career in business after graduation. Of students who became members of the party, he said, "They don't know anything about the political realities in China. They just want to improve their own positions and so they follow the trend. I can assure you that if they spent just one day in my family they would know that all this [political rhetoric] is nonsense. In China there are big problems with corruption. I know this for a fact." Hu went on to say that there were many instances of party members whose children had been admitted to universities despite mediocre educational results, and even cases in which party members had been able to buy degrees for their children.

When talking about the blocking of university intranets, Hu said that he found the censorship offensive and it made him both angry and sad. He had no faith in politics, he said, as he found party members to be corrupt and focused on their own individual interests. He mentioned that he had downloaded illegal videos of the 1989 Tiananmen incident and that it was a problem that the government had never admitted its wrongdoing. "The government treats its citizens like infants without memory," he said. It surprised me that Hu talked about what is generally held to be a very sensitive political issue in such direct terms, and as he spoke I was about to turn off my tape recorder. But he intervened and said that there was no need for me to do so. He said that he was not afraid to talk about political issues. He considered this to be a human right.

He also told me that he and his girlfriend had been together since high school and that to begin with his parents had been worried about their relationship. "At first my parents didn't accept my girlfriend because they didn't know her family and didn't know a lot about her. They also thought that I would waste my time with her and become careless about studying. But I just brought her to meet my father, and he accepted her and gradually came to like her."

When I later asked Mandy to help me transcribe some of my interviews, I was uncertain whether to give her this tape, though I finally decided to do so, despite my uneasiness about the politically sensitive material it contained. As always, I stressed that the interview was absolutely confidential. When Mandy had finished working on the recorded interview, we discussed it, and she said that this person seemed so remarkable and attractive that she had almost fallen in love with his voice. She was impressed with the confident way in which he spoke and about how he had confronted his father in relation to his right to choose his own girlfriend. However, she said that there was a part of the recording she did not understand. What was he referring to when he mentioned the Chinese army, Tiananmen, and 1989? To say that this was an awkward moment would be a gross understatement. I very much regretted having given her the tape, though now that she had asked me about what was on it, I told her briefly what is well known outside of China.[8] An odd silence followed, and we both tried to change the subject as quickly as possible.

A Blocked Oedipal Project?

The stories recounted above suggest that there is an unresolved existential tension between the patriarchal control of the state and a desire for autonomy, and that people address this tension imaginatively in different ways. The confrontational attitude of Hu, the Beijing University student, as he argued that freedom of speech is a human right, and the quite different attitude of Wu Liang, the Tsinghua University student, who regarded censorship as justified or unjustified depending on whether it was for the common good, exemplify the general stereotypical counter-images that Tsinghua students and Beijing University students hold of each other. Students of both universities construe their university vis-à-vis the other. Students of Tsinghua University say, "Beijing University students talk as if they were leaders, but they do not act." Beijing University students respond to this by saying, "[Tsinghua students] are just doing what they are told." These political images have their sexual counterparts. It is commonly held, by students of both universities, that "Tsinghua students live like monks." This sarcasm is spurred by the fact that there are few female students at Tsinghua, but it also mirrors the idea that the students do what they are supposed to do rather than playing around. By contrast, among Tsinghua students there are countless fantasies about the girls at Beijing University. The stereotype is that Beijing University girls are prettier than the science girls of Tsinghua. One Tsinghua girl told me that Beijing University girls live like the characters in the American sitcom *Sex and the City*, referring to some girls that she knew who used makeup and were forever changing boyfriends.

To what extent do students of these two universities actually conform to these opposing stereotypes? What interests me is that they represent two images of the Chinese elite, and reflect contrasting ways in which the state is imagined. Would it be too far-fetched to suggest that the students imaginatively play out the oedipal project, which has been blocked in relation to parents and state, among themselves? When action is blocked, people have recourse to fantasies, imaginatively attempting to change a situation that cannot be objectively changed. According to Michael Jackson, "Play enables us to renegotiate the given, experiment with alternatives, imagine how things might be otherwise, and so resolve obliquely and artificially that which cannot be solved in the 'real' world" (Jackson 1998:29). In the foregoing student narratives, the stereotype of a diligent and law-abiding Tsinghua University is congruent with the government's will to silence criticism and restore a harmonious society. The narrative here is one of identifying with (former) President Hu Jintao, who in fact graduated from Tsinghua, and supporting the government's attempts to sustain social order. By contrast, Beijing University students represent the potentially rebellious child who may challenge parental authority.

Perhaps a difference between what can broadly be termed a science-oriented outlook and a liberal arts outlook plays a role in shaping different orientations regarding what aspirations students have and what constitutes the good life. Students of the humanities tend to believe that the government prefers Chinese youth to study sciences rather than arts, since in this way they can be more easily persuaded not to ask the wrong kinds of questions. Even though my interlocutors always stressed that both Beijing and Tsinghua were "top" universities, there was also a form of competition going on between them, and it is hard to ignore the fact that the Chinese government is made up primarily of engineers, including a great number of Tsinghua graduates.

If the state evokes images of both care and control (Hage 1996a:472–477), it seems that the Chinese state is imagined through both the life-giving love epitomized in the notion of filial obligation and a repressive form of parental love. This was powerfully brought home to me by the comments of Chinese author and critic of China's political system Liao Yiwu. In an interview with Martin Gøttske in the Danish newspaper *Information*, fifty-year-old Liao Yiwu says that he was "reborn" on the fourth of June 1989, when the Communist Party violently repressed the protesters in Beijing's Tiananmen Square: "Then I was a poet and I primarily wrote surreal poems. I thought I didn't have to worry about social reality and to be interested in politics, the society and ordinary people. But then they started shooting around Tiananmen Square. It drew a line in the sand, a line which for me marks life before and after . . . I changed from being indifferent to being incredibly angry."

He wrote a poem about this event called "The Massacre," after which, in the eyes of the state, he changed from being a poet to being a criminal, and was imprisoned. Before that happened, he had won several literary prizes and was a celebrated artist within the official literary system. During his four years in prison he was tortured and twice attempted suicide. He was released in 1994, but still feels that he is in prison within China's borders. "Even though I was released several years ago, I am still caught in an invisible prison," he told me. During the twenty-year anniversary of the Tiananmen incident, Liao Yiwu noticed that he was under more intensive surveillance. The metaphors he uses to phrase his anger and resentment include images of having been robbed of life, and of the government/party/nation as a domineering parent:

The motherland must really love me a lot since she hits me so much. I do not love her at all, but she loves me so much. The system is like a mother who desperately tries to make the child behave correctly by constantly slapping it. But I am no longer a child. If the system does not change, I am afraid that when I am eighty years old, the motherland will still see me as a little child it should punish . . . In my view Chinese society will have improved significantly the day the motherland decides to give me a passport, allows me to leave the country and stops loving me so damn much.

Perspectives

In China family images seem to pervade all spheres of social life, including the state's relationship with its citizens. While teachers serve as mediators here, some teachers, such as Jia Ling, can be seen as trickster figures representing the allure of the foreign and questioning the idea of a paternal state. But it is important to note that not all students find such political questions as the blocking of Water Wood or the silencing of the Tiananmen incident, to be equally significant in their lives. Some, like Mandy, were in fact unaware of the latter incident. What is important here is that the party ceases to be imagined as a parent figure exercising "control as care" or making hard choices that sustain the common good (*da wo*). Control comes to be viewed as unjustified.

Liao Yiwu's account is paradigmatic in describing an experience of the Chinese state, which he merges with the motherland as a repressive mother figure whose will stands in the way of the child/citizen growing up and coming into his own, withholding his ability to express himself, obtain a passport, and leave the country. Hu's comment about the closing of Water Wood led him to talk about the trauma of Tiananmen in similar terms, saying that the government treats the general populace "like infants without memory." As I have shown, 1989 represents a trauma in Chinese history that is absent from public discourse and rarely enters into private conversations. This trauma constitutes a form of collective amnesia, and also reflects an informal contract between parents and the state that keeps parents from passing on knowledge of such historical events to their children. In this way, the state is imagined as a parental figure exercising social control, blocking students' ability to communicate with students outside China, and keen to ensure that a form of rebellion like the one that took place in 1989 will not happen again.

Even though the 1989 Tiananmen incident has largely been construed in the West as springing from a desire for human rights, it was also precipitated by a shortage of jobs and frustration experienced by both China's impoverished rural population and a first generation of highly educated Chinese who were caught in a mismatch between their expectations and the actual opportunities for upward social mobility. For students like Wu Liang, joining the party was tied to a pragmatic project of social mobility and a way of generating a path to adulthood.

Chapter 4

Between Parents, Party, and Peers

"MY FATHER WAS SO PROUD OF ME when I became a member of the party," Wu Liang told me. "He was also proud when I entered Tsinghua. For him, becoming a party member was really something great."

Wu and his father shared an interest in Chinese history, and since he was a little boy his father had told him stories about the achievements of the Communist Party. In this respect, Wu Liang's experience of growing up closely resembles Yan's depiction of an older villager who recalled suddenly being taken seriously when he joined the Communist Party (Yan 1999:85).

About one-fifth of the students of Tsinghua and Beijing University are members of the party, and those students who were not members often expressed mixed feelings about those who were. While some felt that being a member of the party was necessary in order to become highly respected and successful, others found party members to be either opportunistic or naive, or both. These ambivalent attitudes mirror Stig Thøgersen's framing of party members as "parasites or civilizers." Whereas party cadres see themselves as part of a civilizing mission, peasants sometimes define them as parasites, living illegitimately off the labor of the rural population (Thøgersen 2003:192).

I now turn to what is at stake for students who become members of the Communist Party. What does it mean to be a Communist in contemporary China? What is the relationship between loyalty to one's family and loyalty to the party? And what can the issue of party membership tell us about social differences in China?

Deng Xiaoping replaced Mao's slogans with his own: "It does not matter whether the cat is black or white as long as it catches mice," and "It is glorious to become rich." He saw the need for a strong private market, though strictly controlled by the Communist Party. Deng's vision of utopia borrowed extensively from Asian models, especially Singapore's version of Confucian capitalism

(Buruma 2003:17). One of the major consequences of expanding capitalism in alliance with a strong state has been the introduction by Hu Jintao and Wen Jiabao of various policy adjustments to promote a "harmonious society" (*hexie shehui*)—in other words, to address the negative consequences of the increasing polarization of society. Since the reform era, there has been a "rehabilitation" of Confucius and Confucianism in order to give moral legitimacy to the party. Furthermore, a constant topic of discussion is the extent to which family loyalties and filial obligations can contribute to China's economic development, as they have for the so-called "Asian tigers": it has not escaped the attention of China's leaders and the general public that Taiwan, Singapore, and Hong Kong have developed rapidly while continuing to emphasize Confucian family values, and much the same could be said for Japan and South Korea (M. K. Whyte 1997:23).

In his book *The Good Communist*, Frank Pieke describes how government officials are trained for placement in the Communist Party and how this process is full of contradictions (Pieke 2009). Pieke shows that while the CCP has undergone radical transformation since the revolutionary years under Mao, the party is still dependent upon ideologically committed and loyal cadres, selected through a highly rigorous process. Pieke also points out that "China's administration is Mao Zedong's worst nightmare become real." Rather than being directly involved in the life and work of the masses, cadres have become a ruling elite who worship book learning and formal education. Pieke also notes that "the learning, discipline and privilege that cadre training provides is a key transformative experience in the construction of cadres' unique sense of personhood, a sense of self that straddles the boundaries between strong individuality, total submission to the party's will, elitist exclusivity and faceless anonymity." In other words, Pieke suggests that party membership involves managing contradictory social imperatives.

In *Deep China*, Kleinman and colleagues (2011) explore the psychology of Chinese citizens. The authors argue that China's extraordinarily rapid modernization "may have created a special cultural version of the divided self" (23). They invoke a famous painting by the Chinese artist Huang Youngyu of an owl with one eye closed and the other open, a pose that has been interpreted as a critical wink at the terrible period of the Cultural Revolution. The authors of *Deep China* argue that this image also reveals a truth about contemporary China, namely "a deep structural tension in China's moral worlds and in the Chinese individual" (23), who variously experiences a split between actual social practice and an inner world of contemplation, and thus struggles to keep one eye open and the other closed. When reading this account I was struck by the degree to which it spoke to the tensions among both those of my interlocutors who are party members and those who are not.

Doing fieldwork "in the footsteps of the Communist Party" poses certain methodological challenges (Hansen 2006:81). I was not allowed to attend party meetings, which are closed to outsiders, and so I had to rely on students' informal accounts of what takes place there. I was told that when a person is selected as a potential member of the party and the person also aspires to become one, he or she goes through a period in which his or her actions and character are closely observed. This is sometimes referred to as "the engagement process." During this period the person writes an application, which is an expression of his or her motivation for joining the party and of his or her willingness to make sacrifices for the country and for the party. When a person is found to be suitable in terms of political thought and moral character, he or she may be selected for membership. This is popularly referred to as "marriage." In this way party membership is phrased as a process of growing up, and of gaining recognition from significant others in positions of authority. In other words, a person changes from being a child of the state to being recognized not only as a grown-up person but as an exemplary individual, a model for others to follow. As Wu Liang told me, "We have to be role models, guiding the actions and thoughts of others."

As a party member, one is expected to serve as an example to others and to take part in meetings once a week, or every two weeks, in which party members study the work of Zhou Enlai, Deng Xiaoping, and Mao Zedong and discuss current affairs of the country and matters related to the university more broadly, including attempts at reforming the educational system. Catherine, a member of the party at Tsinghua University, also told me that at the most recent party meeting she had attended, suicide had been the topic of the discussion, with members trying to work out ways of changing the educational system so as to prevent more such tragic cases.

As a party member, one takes charge of the recruitment of new members. "What are the possibilities of divorce?" I asked Wu Liang. He had not given this issue much thought and had no clear idea what would happen if a person were to leave the party. I found this to be the case for all the party members I interviewed. However, in sharing her thoughts on this issue, Jia Ling (my teacher friend) told me that many students were naive with respect to the seriousnsess of joining the party: "Young people may find themselves in a very difficult situation if they join the party and wish to leave it. They will be subjected to intensive persuasion and pressure. Leaving the party may end up damaging their reputation, and they will be worse off than if they had never joined the party in the first place."

So what are young people's motivations for joining the party? I will try to answer this question by moving beyond official rhetoric and focusing on the stories of three different students whose aspirations for party membership were tied to a project of self-development rather than a wish to make sacrifices to their country.

Party Membership as Self-development

When I arrived by bicycle at the West Gate of Tsinghua University one cold and hazy afternoon during the winter of 2005, I spotted Wu Liang from a distance, a thin guy wearing glasses who looked frail in his overlarge winter coat. I apologized for being a few minutes late, and he noted that it was a habit for Tsinghua students to be on time. He commented that his friend Helen had told him that I was "a bit shy." He went on to tell me that he had been shy himself but had overcome this inhibition. He said that he was in fact unique since he fully understood that "being on top means everything" and that this was something he continued to struggle for. He had "high aims in life."

As we sat opposite each other at an off-campus café, Wu flashed a shy smile and confessed that this was his first time off campus that semester, and the first time he had tasted a cappuccino. When he opened his notebook, I complimented his beautiful handwriting. He explained that he was very passionate about Chinese calligraphy and in particular loved the poetry of the Tang dynasty.

When I asked him about his family background, he told me that his parents were factory workers from a suburb of Shanghai. Having this background and having entered Tsinghua (only a hundred out of 300,000 applicants are accepted by the economics faculty there), he felt that he had already "achieved something really great."

Some way into our conversation, Wu talked about how his mother had "educated him with a stick," keeping him from playing with friends, watching television, or playing games. As a child he had been quite lonely. He said that he had learned to love his parents by being friends with girls who were devoted to their parents. These girls had explained to him that his parents really did love him, which was why they were treating him harshly, disciplining him, and urging him to focus on studying. Now, he said, he was grateful to his parents, since by being forced to study he had been able to enter Tsinghua. His parents had hoped he would enter Fudan University in Shanghai, but he had surpassed their expectations, and he now realized that being at the highest level was extremely important. He added that he was a "unique" student in the sense that he was not primarily struggling to get a high GPA. He was genuinely interested in studying, and he read many books outside his economics curriculum. He was interested in Western philosophy and literature, and he also wrote fiction. He said that he worked on finding ways to manage his time and had become used to sleeping very little as a way of saving time and accommodating the many things he wanted to do in life.

As previously mentioned, Wu's father was really proud of him when he became a party member. His father had told him stories about the achievements of the party. In particular he remembered his father's account of Mao's long march and the stories of the national hero, Lei Feng, who sacrificed his own well-being for the country. Wu Liang explained that his father had passed on to him his love for the party and the motherland. He emphasized that he truly believed in communism, as opposed to many party members who join the party for opportunistic reasons, such as to obtain a good recommendation from a teacher, a scholarship abroad, or ultimately a position within the state bureaucracy. He found that China's problems had to do with the current phase of economic development and saw the building of a strong economy as China's most important political project. Only through the building of a strong economy could China restore the power it had had in the past, and cease to be looked down upon by Western countries. Moreover, in the process of building a strong economy, the gap between rural and urban China would eventually shrink.

Wu emphasized the need to improve oneself constantly, and his dedication to "work selflessly for others" echoed party rhetoric. His friend Helen, who had introduced us to each other, had also told me that Wu was in fact quite remarkable in this respect. He took his responsibility to others very seriously and sometimes spent time helping other students with their assignments. Even though he used the language of sacrifice, being a party member seemed like a very individual project, related to a struggle for distinction, or *suzhi*.

When I cautiously asked him if he had a girlfriend, I thought I was perhaps being too personal, and his self-ironic answer took me by surprise.

I am afraid I am not excellent enough. You see, there are so few girls at Tsinghua, so the competition in this respect is very fierce. In fact, my mother is always talking about this. She wants me to find a nice girl, someone who is sweet and gentle [*wen rou*], but my requirements are higher than [those of] my parents. I want her actually to accept my thoughts and I find it important that we can talk about life and also children. I want to see my children grow up to become distinguished people, not necessarily rich, but in personality and virtue. If I meet someone who only cares about money, I will consider this relationship to be doomed. In fact all girls say that they do not care about money or power, but actually the society is quite cruel to everyone, and eventually many women . . . many people will surrender to this trend. Maybe I may even eventually surrender to this trend.

Wu said that he wanted to be a "quiet person in the society," an expression that suggested the ideal of the Confucian scholar-official, yet with a competitive edge, since he later told me that his ambition was to become the first Chinese professor at Tsinghua within the particular field of economics that he was studying, a position that had until now always been held by professors from the United States. He added that this was a very high goal to set for himself, but he was quite confident that he would succeed if he worked hard enough.

When I returned to Beijing during the spring of 2007 for the second part of my fieldwork, I tried for some time to contact Wu Liang, but he did not respond to any of my messages. One day he called me and asked me out for lunch. I could hardly recognize him. He looked more mature and was wearing a light blue business suit. He had picked out a Japanese restaurant, and as we made our way past the hawkers who were crowding the pavement in the Wudaokou area, we tried to talk over the noise of cars and music playing in the restaurants and shops we passed. Wu was keen to tell me that he had received a scholarship to go to UCLA to study for a Ph.D. in economics.

Over lunch he told me that he had changed his perception of many things. In the past, he had pursued a philosophical approach to economic theory. But now he saw things in a more pragmatic way. He had realized the importance of making money. "Without money, one is powerless in China," he said. When I asked him about issues related to social inequality, which he had seemed passionate about before, he seemed uninterested and changed the subject. He was more interested in telling me about an idea of his that had impressed an influential professor who had then helped him with recommendations for his application to graduate school. "What was your idea about?" I asked. "Toothpaste," he said.[1]

Wu Liang also told me that he had a girlfriend whom he considered beautiful, but more importantly, she was very smart. He found this to be the most important quality in a person. He said that she had received the highest grade in her provincial college entrance examinations, and that she was also going to the United States to do a Ph.D. Knowing that many of the students who were going abroad to study were worried about the long separations they had to endure from boyfriends, girlfriends, and family, I told him that he was very fortunate that they would be going abroad together. When I asked him whether he planned to return to China after obtaining his doctorate, he said that he was not sure. I never managed to meet his girlfriend, and I eventually found myself wondering whether she had been invented to impress upon me an image of success.

For Wu Liang, party membership was initially tied to winning the respect and recognition of his father, who emphasized the merits of the Communist Party in transforming China from a poor agricultural society with a small elite controlling the masses to a more egalitarian society in which his son had now, through hard work, been able to enter the top university in the country and become a member of the party. For Wu Liang's father, becoming a member of the party was a major accomplishment. However, having entered the party and in a sense "become the party," Wu Liang had become disillusioned and lost faith in its ideals, which were incompatible with his new realization that money was a prerequisite for having any power or voice in China. His dream of becoming the first Chinese professor within a specific field of economics was transformed into a dream of migrating to the United States and making money.

A Stranger in the City

One chilly spring morning in 2005 I decided to take a break from fieldwork, and was sitting at a French sidewalk café in Beijing's Sanlitun neighbourhood, where I had lived as a child. As I was drinking coffee and jotting down notes, I was distracted by a mynah bird in an antique birdcage hanging in a tree above me. It was crying out "hello" and "*ni hao*" interchangeably when a waiter, a young man with a broad smile and lively eyes, noticed my interest in the bird and asked me in English where I was from. After I told him about my Ph.D. project on Chinese university students, we exchanged phone numbers.

Bai Gang's parents were peasants who worked in the fields and had sacrificed a lot in order to enable him, as the younger son, to receive a university education. He had a brother and a sister. In their rural area two children had been authorized, but when his mother became pregnant a third time, they chose to have a third child and to pay a fine. It had taken his parents five years of hard work and saving to pay back the money they had borrowed from different family members and friends for the fine. Bai Gang spoke very caringly about his parents and said he greatly respected them. He talked mostly of his mother, who he said was a very intelligent woman, even though she was not well educated. He said that she would often tease him by saying that he had been a very expensive child.

Like other students from rural areas, Bai Gang and his parents lived in different worlds: "My parents have never been to Beijing," he said. "They don't know much about the world. Their lives are about working and saving money for their children. Like other traditional farmers, what they care most about is money. They work so hard that they even sacrifice their own health for money. They don't even care about spending the money. They don't trust banks, so they hide their money."

Bai Gang talked about how he and his brother tried to make small investments from the money they earned. His brother worked as a cook in Sanlitun, and he had helped Bai Gang also find a part-time job in this area. They tried to persuade their parents to invest some of their money, but were unable to do so. "This is a generation gap," he said. Furthermore, having experienced the world outside his village, he was drawn to the opportunities of urban life, the allure of modernity. Whereas his parents were concerned with obtaining a basic sense of security, he thought that there was "more to life than money." He yearned to travel to foreign countries and experience more of life. Even though being a waiter cut into his study time (in his view, disadvantaged poor rural students like himself could only spend 70 percent of their time studying), he welcomed the opportunity to practice speaking English with the foreigners who frequented the café and catch glimpses of another way of life.

During our conversations, Bai Gang always returned to the issue of social differences as they were played out between students at the university and the "*hukou* question." *Hukou* is the household registration system, which in effect means that there are different forms of citizenship in China. People cannot move freely about the country, and rural students have a temporary residence permit in Beijing that is valid only for as long as they are studying. If they cannot find a job after graduation, in which their employer can "arrange a *hukou* for them," they must, at least in principle, return to their home provinces. If they stay, they become part of the so-called "floating population" of millions of migrants living without legal rights as "strangers in the city" (Zhang 2001). Thus students with a rural background are handicapped in their struggle to transcend their rural status.

Bai Gang also mentioned the fact that, by contrast with students from the provinces, students from Beijing can enter universities with inferior degrees. A double standard exists. Though non-Beijing residents are respected for their higher grades, they tend to be looked down upon, since they lack other kinds of social capital. Bai Gang put it this way as we chatted in an off-campus café:

For instance, this is the first time for me to go to a café. Maybe the students from Beijing have a more open mind because they are accustomed to modern life. For example, the Internet, eating in cafés, in modern restaurants, their ability in painting, dancing, music ... But many students from the rural areas don't have access to this, so there is a gap between the cities and the rural areas.... Sometimes they look down upon us because they have grown up in the capital and feel that they have an advanced attitude. For people from the rural areas this leads to a lack of confidence because we live in a modern city but we are from less developed areas.

Andrew Kipnis has argued that *suzhi* discourse emphasizes rather than denies structural differences(Kipnis 2007:389).[2] The comments of Professor Wen, a teacher at Tsinghua, support this view. Professor Wen explained to me that students from the countryside were often very diligent but in other respects they were in fact no better than Beijing students who had been exposed to other aspects of life and had been more developed from early childhood. By this he meant that they were accustomed to urban life and thus had a higher *suzhi*. However, from Bai Gang's point of view, it was unfair that students who were not Beijing residents had to have higher scores in order to be admitted to elite universities in Beijing.

Bai Gang's perceived lack of confidence in relation to urban students, who were accustomed to "modern" forms of consumption and distinction, can be likened to the difficulty of a migrant adjusting fully to the norms of the host society. Even though Bai Gang found most students from Beijing to be "friendly," he confessed to feeling estranged from them, like an outsider struggling to be accepted as an equal. Clearly a feeling of inferiority, reflecting a lack of equal rights, went hand in hand with a sense of having to change one's sense of self in order to acquire more *suzhi*. Although Bai Gang himself did not use the term *suzhi*, since this would stigmatize him even more, his comments on having "an open mind," on being accustomed to "modern life," and the value he placed on consumption patterns and artistic abilities, all clearly mirror *suzhi* discourse.

Bai Gang said that in some ways, he sympathized with Ma Jia Jue, a Yunnan University student from rural Guanxi province, who killed four of his fellow students after a dispute over a card game, in which they accused him of cheating. Bai Gang thought Ma Jia Jue probably felt demeaned by his poor rural origins. This story powerfully brings home the great importance of social differences to students who live closely together in university dormitories.[3]

Ghostly Doubles

It was during the winter of 2004 that Ma Jia Jue committed the murders, then fled. When I was in Shanghai, pictures of him were posted all over town and a manhunt was under way. People speculated about his whereabouts and his motives until finally he was caught on the island of Hainan in the south of China and subsequently executed. He had refused legal defense and declared that he wanted to die. Much speculation took place as to what drove a young university student to commit such a crime. He himself said on national television that he wanted to seek revenge on his fellow students, who had looked down on him because he was poor. Ma Jia Jue had been subjected to various forms of taunts because he dressed unfashionably, and on one occasion someone urinated on his bed.

Like Bai Gang, Ma Jia Jue was from a peasant family in Guanxi province and had helped his parents with farmwork since he was five. While at university he had never asked his parents for money, but would wash the clothes of his roommates for a few yuan. His family had borrowed his entire 5,000 yuan tuition from the school, and while he was waiting for a state stipend he would cut classes because he had no shoes to wear. However, he had always been an exceptionally bright student and had won the national physics competition. He had also won third prize in the national mathematics competition. Most of my interlocutors agreed that only a mentally disturbed person could commit such crimes, but those from rural families, like Bai Gang, stressed that the crux of the conflict was his poor peasant background. Ma Jia Jue had reacted so violently because his peers had called him a cheat and looked down upon him.

In a thought-provoking article titled "The Corporeal Politics of Quality (*Suzhi*)," Ann Anagnost describes the migrant and the urban middle-class child as "ghostly doubles" and makes the somewhat curious argument that value is abstracted from the laboring bodies of migrants and placed into the bodies of urban middle-class children (Anagnost 2004:191).[4]

Anagnost's juxtaposition of the migrant and the middle-class child as "ghostly doubles" is a powerful image, and helpful in understanding what is at stake for students, like Ma Jia Jue, who attempt to cross the rural-urban divide. Nevertheless, Anagnost's interpretation of the production and significance of social differences through "a rhetoric and practice of separation" that is "stunningly concretized by the construction of new gated communities away from the 'ghettoes of the poor'" (Anagnost 2004:190–191) overlooks the ways in which, in some instances, the rural migrant and the urban (middle-class) child are not necessarily separated. On the contrary, they sometimes participate in the same educational system, live close together in small dormitories, and compete against each other, though on unequal terms. In the cases of Ma Jia Jue and Bai Gang, the migrant and the (middle-class) child are in fact embodied in the same person.

One day, Bai Gang told me that he was preparing to become a member of the Communist Party and that this decision was tied to precisely this strategy of seeking to transcend his rural status:

In fact, I might become a member of the Communist Party before my graduation. I don't think I will be so conscious of being a member of the party, but I plan to become a member because it will be helpful in order to find a job in the future. Especially if you want to work within a government institution you have to, and this is sometimes written in job advertisements—they call for being a member of the Communist Party. I think this is a good thing for me because there is serious competition for jobs. I handed in my application in 2003, after the SARS epidemic, because I did well in school during this period and because my teacher noticed that I took on some responsibility in connection with the practical matters during the internment period, and therefore my teacher asked me whether I would like to join the party. If it hadn't been for SARS I probably wouldn't have had this kind of opportunity.

Bai Gang implies that party membership is not something one chooses, but rather something one is chosen for. However, since Bai Gang comes from a poor rural background with no official connections, his commitment to join the party is primarily a strategy for improving his chances in the labor market after graduation. His primary concern is to be able to get a good job in an "opportunity city" (Beijing, Shanghai, Guangzhou, or Shenzhen) and to obtain an urban *hukou*, a residence permit.

Even though he said that he would not be so "conscious of becoming a party member," when I asked him more about what becoming a member of the party entailed, he responded using the party rhetoric of self-sacrifice:

You should have selfless dedication, and work for the country, work for the people. You must improve yourself constantly. As a member, you should strengthen your skills and be an example of an advanced mind. And in a group, you should strive to be the most advanced. If someone is in trouble, you should help him selflessly. I think this norm will be good for me to strive for, as it would really be good for any person, whether he is a member of the Communist Party or not. It would be good for every citizen to have this spirit.

For Bai Gang, becoming a member of the party was primarily a matter of self-interest, a strategy for upward mobility. This brings me back to the tension between the struggle to strike a balance between autonomy and dependence. Ferguson points out the difference between "social inequalities" and "asocial inequalities" when describing the tribulations of unemployed black South Africans, noting that "those suffering from asocial inequality increasingly seek out social inequality" (Ferguson 2013:233). This logic of "if you can't beat them, join them" appeared to be at the heart of Bai Gang's strategy of joining the party. By seeking to belong to the party, he hoped to escape his position of being an outsider in Beijing—preferring to *belong* to someone and surrender some of his autonomy rather than to be no one.

Nevertheless, at this point he did not appear to see any moral quandary arising from this contradiction. On the contrary, he was proud of having been chosen for party membership by a respected teacher, and it seemed to be a win-win situation. Becoming a party member, he hoped, would increase his chances of finding a well-paid job and obtaining an urban Beijing residence permit (*hukou*). In this way, he also expected to fulfill the generational contract, to send remittances back to his parents and his less-fortunate brother and sister, since, after all, he had been the youngest and the luckiest child. The family had devoted many resources to ensuring that he could receive a university education. The idea of returning to rural Guangxi to live with them and take care of his parents during their old age was very remote. Bai Gang thought that he could contribute more to the entire family by finding a good job in Beijing.[5]

However, Bai Gang admitted that his parents were not too impressed with his becoming a party member. Like many other villagers, they were frustrated with the corruption of local officials, who taxed their crops heavily, and they commented cynically on the sons of cadres who would conspicuously return home driving luxury cars. "My parents miss Chairman Mao because Mao cared about the peasants of China, unlike the current party members, who are busy filling their own pockets," he said, noting that they had a picture of Chairman Mao in their living room and would burn incense for him along with the other ancestors. He said this with a compassionate smile, indicating that he found this practice to be out of touch with reality, although he shared his parents' frustration over the corruption of government officials and the widening disparity between China's booming urban coastal areas and the poverty-stricken countryside.

Stuck in the Ant Tribe

When I met Bai Gang again during the second part of my fieldwork, in 2007, he seemed more disillusioned than the cheerful boy of two years earlier. He had recently graduated and was looking for a job in Beijing. He also said that he felt stuck at a dead end, since people with a bachelor's degree earn only 1,500 yuan a month and those with a graduate degree as little as 2,000 yuan. This level of income makes it hard to settle permanently in Beijing, find a place to live, provide for a family, and send remittances back to one's parents and siblings. Although he knew he could probably easily get a job in another part of China, closer to home, he was unwilling to give up the idea of making a life for himself in Beijing.

He was deeply distressed by what he experienced as the increasing corruption in society in general and within the educational system in particular. He mentioned a friend of his, whose father had strong personal connections to a high-ranking party official. Through this powerful connection he was promised a position the following year even though he did not really live up to the formal requirements. According to Bai Gang, his friend now spends a year on campus without doing anything and is going out to bars in the evenings and spending his time simply playing around (*wan*) with his girlfriend.[6]

As for his commitment to the work of the party, Bai Gang said that he now helped with recruitment of new members from among university students. "This procedure is equally corrupt," he said. "What happens is that we recommend our friends. In principle we are supposed to observe them, hold meetings and discuss their assets and flaws, but this is done superficially. It is all about connections [*guanxi*]." By becoming a party member, Bai Gang in a sense "became the party"—a part of a structural logic whereby connections were far more important than values and virtues. As for his own case, he had assisted in recruiting new members, but his party membership had not provided a means of social mobility.

In his book *China's Ant Tribe*, Lian Si coins the term "ant tribe" to describe the problem of rising unemployment in China among college graduates. He argues that many unemployed students share the fate of China's many migrant workers: living in lousy conditions on the outskirts of a city, with low-income jobs or no income at all, yet reluctant to give up the dream of finding work, and finding it too shameful to return to their hometowns empty-handed (Si 2009). Explaining his imagery, Si notes: "Bees, as they fly, give the impression of upward mobility, while ants are always seen as down on earth, stuck to the ground." His book title reflects the resemblance between intelligent, industrious, yet anonymous and underpaid graduates and ants. Because of the soaring number of unemployed university graduates without a Beijing *hukou*, Bai Gang's aspirations to secure a job in Beijing were continually unsuccessful, even though he was a party member.

Keeping Various Paths Open

Using Lian Si's terminology, one might say that if Lu Gang resembled an ant, Zhou Lemin was more like a bee. Zhou had suggested we could meet briefly by the sports track at Tsinghua University, since he had a very tight schedule. Every semester hundreds of Tsinghua students gather at the dusty running track to take part in the running event of the university. The slogan "Study healthily for the motherland for the next fifty years" is visible on large red banners. Boys have to be able to run 3,000 meters in fifteen minutes, while for girls the requirement is 1,500 meters. Most students dread this exercise, though few find it difficult to complete.

It took me a while to recognize Zhou in his green tracksuit. Normally he dressed in a blue velvet suit and wore large-rimmed spectacles, making him stand out among the typically more casually dressed college students. But today he blended in with the crowd. Having stretched out his sore legs and put his glasses back on, he told me:

In fact I find this exercise annoying because it is too inflexible. I think the requirement to be fit and healthy is OK, but there should be more flexibility in the planning of the event. Actually I had to do some work for a company today, where I am working as an intern, but I had to cancel. My boss found this hard to understand. A running exercise? So it was a dilemma for me, but I HAVE to show up, otherwise I will be punished. And as a member of the party, we have to do these things in an enthusiastic way. We have to be a model for others.

This may be taken as a concrete example of the contradictions of *suzhi jioayu*, which I will explore in more detail in Chapter 5. The requirement to take part in a collective running exercise, in which the body of the individual person is supposed to represent the body politic by being strong and healthy, clashed with the requirement to improve one's "social skills" as an intern in a foreign company, a context in which one was expected to be a flexible and autonomous person, responsive to the needs of a competitive market economy.

Zhou Lemin's background was, in his own words, "quite unique." "What I mean is, I am neither from rural nor urban China, and even though I have grown up during the Period of Opening Up and Reform, I have grown up under communism." Zhou Lemin went on to explain how he had grown up in an oil field in a part of Shenzhen with many state-owned oil companies. This area continued to function as a *dan wei*, a work unit, that until 1998 provided for the families of workers, at which time prime minister Zhu Rongji came to power and partly privatized the state-owned companies. There was a rationing system whereby people would queue up for eggs at 4:00 p.m., and for soap the following day. At 5:00 p.m., people went to the water station. Zhou had fond memories of his childhood when "everybody had what they needed." He emphasized that this area was sparsely populated because of the poor quality of the soil, but people were quite prosperous because of the oil industry, and they continue to be granted state pensions.

Being a *bei nan dang*, a member of the party, and a master's student in international relations, with parents who were wealthy and well-connected party members, Zhou had already established himself in his own apartment in Beijing. He said that he was aware that he was in a fortunate position, and that having good "material conditions" (*tiaojian*) also made him an attractive marriage partner. His dream was to enter the foreign ministry and to work as a diplomat in foreign countries.

Although he found the running exercise tedious, it was, in his own words, "a small sacrifice to make." Zhou Lemin pretended to be making sacrifices for his country, though this was, he said bluntly, mere rhetoric. He explained that the procedure for obtaining party membership was a masquerade. Having parents who are party members was something that was "helpful" if one wanted to join the party. "There is a more or less standard way of writing these applications, all the stuff about making sacrifices for the country," Zhou said. He was a member of the party for strategic reasons, as were other party members, he believed. "That is just the way the system works, and if you want to join the foreign ministry this is the road you have to take."

Notice the contrast between the egalitarian simple life that he associated with the communism he grew up with and the position as a party member, which had become an element of his personal striving for an elite status. He seemed to have moved with the changing times, and therefore he did not view these alternatives as contradictory. Rather, it seemed that he and his family had adapted to and derived advantage from the political and economic changes; his parents had been able to help pass on elite status to their son, including party membership. Zhou Lemin was both a party member and an intern in a foreign company, and in this way he seemed to keep various paths open and present himself as very confident about his own future.

As Zhou Lemin's comments indicate, becoming a party member was a strategic choice, one that did not seem problematic to him, even though he did not "believe in communism." It is possible that there are many people like Zhou, for whom the party has represented the interests of the Chinese elite to a substantial degree. Rosen has analyzed issues of party recruitment from the perspective of those being recruited and found that China's youth cohort sees party membership as an avenue to opportunities within a competitive job market (Rosen 2004). However, even though this mostly quantitative work confirms that the Chinese elite support the party, the autobiographical sketches in this chapter highlight the ambiguities in how this support is *experienced*. Although there is no political alternative to the Communist Party, and even though party membership is pursued as a strategic choice, Zhou Lemin's reflections reveal a certain ironic distance from empty ideals. One day he told me a joke that goes, "What is the meaning of communism in China? The answer is: The longest and most difficult road to capitalism."

Perspectives

My interlocutors each experienced in his own way a tension between party, parents, and peers, though this was something they voiced privately to me and never publicly declared. This contrast between private and public does not necessarily imply a "cultural version of the divided self" (Kleinman et al.), and unlike Kleinman, I do not see it as a uniquely Chinese phenomenon. The experience of being pulled in different directions is part and parcel of the human condition itself. As Hannah Arendt argues, social life is full of contradictions, and the double binds or tensions between self and other, or between moral ideals and actual lived experience, are never fully or permanently resolved (Arendt 1958 [1998]).

For Bai Gang, becoming a party member was tied to a strategy of trying to transform his rural identity into an urban one, thus making him a fully recognized citizen. In this way he could also grow up in a moral sense in relation to his parents and siblings, and repay them for their sacrifices. His desire to come into his own by working and living in the capital of the country also had to do with a desire not to be looked down upon as a "stranger" and second-class citizen in his own country. However, becoming a party member put him in a double bind, since it was difficult for him to reconcile his belief in the remnants of socialism, which had been part of his rural upbringing by parents who still worshipped Chairman Mao, with what he experienced as the corrupt reality of the party. Rather than sacrifices based on a promise of return, party membership had come to denote mere opportunism and self-interest. He felt disenchanted at seeing himself fall into the role of a corrupt party member, selecting other candidates for party membership because of *guanxi* (connections) rather than because they were motivated or dedicated to pursue the common good. He thought that peasants, like his parents, were paying the highest price for this kind of hypocrisy and moral corruption.

Bai Gang's aspiration to obtain a Beijng *hukou* and thereby transform his status as a rural migrant into that of an urban citizen was what was most pertinently at stake for him. For Wu Liang, whose parents were factory workers on the outskirts of Shanghai, the issue of *hukou* was not a predominant concern, since he already had a *hukou* in a so-called "opportunity city." Rather, his party membership seemed to be part of a project of self-development, an attempt to acquire distinction or *suzhi*. This was suggested when he told me that his party work had helped him overcome his shyness and develop a more confident personality, and in his emphasis on being well-read in both Chinese and foreign literature and philosophy, and his desire to raise children who were noble people of high moral character. When I first met Wu Liang, his project of self-development seemed to be tied to a nationalist project of improving the status of the Chinese nation in the eyes of the world. However, when I met him again, it seemed clear that his personal ambitions of social mobility through migration seemed to have eclipsed his nationalist concerns. This went hand in hand with both a sense of pride at having obtained a scholarship and a sense of disillusionment at the unfairness of the market economy.

Bai Gang's views on becoming a party member changed over the course of his life. Because he embodied both rural and urban China, he initially identified with party rhetoric and its emphasis on social equality, though simultaneously experiencing a split between his sense of obligation to look after his parents and his own desire to lead a cosmopolitan life in Beijing—something he hoped party membership would help him achieve. The sense of division was sharpened by his failure to achieve either goal. He guiltily turned a blind eye to his family and struggled to find new ways to obtain self-realization, neither caring for his parents nor living out his own dreams—stuck, as it were, in China's ant tribe.

I followed Zhou Lemin, Bai Gang, and Wu Liang over the course of a few years and witnessed their gradual disillusionment—their experience that "life was unfair" and that money was needed to survive in a society characterized by increasing inequality rather than by socialist virtues and values. Instead of a hoped-for reciprocation of sacrifices made and future returns, they encountered opportunism and corruption. Nonetheless, as we have seen, their strategies for social mobility played out in radically different ways.

This raises the question of whether the party can continue to sustain legitimacy by proclaiming that love of country and love of party are synonymous if party members seek out personal strategies of social mobility or projects of individual self-development rather than making sacrifices for the common good. People, like Liu Xing, who are not members of the party, tend to emphasize the opportunistic and hypocritical aspects of party membership, arguing that party members merely want a good career. Wu Liang moved from being, in his own words, "a devoted communist" to being disillusioned by widespread party corruption.

Most people admit that self-development is at the heart of their party membership strategies. This view is promoted in both party rhetoric and *suzhi jiaoyu* discourse, highlighting the connection between governing a nation and educating children, as captured in the term *guan*. But to what extent can developing the self and developing the nation go hand in hand?

Chapter 5

The Double Binds of "Education for Quality"

> It is creative appropriation more than anything else that makes the individual feel that life is worth living. Contrasted with this is a relationship to external reality that is one of compliance, the world and its details being recognized, but only as something to be fitted in with or demanding adaptation. Compliance carries with it a sense of futility for the individual and is associated with the idea that nothing matters and that life is not worth living. In a tantalizing way many individuals have experienced just enough of creative living to recognize that for most of their time they are living uncreatively, as if caught up in the creativity of someone else, or of a machine.
>
> —Winnicott (1971) 2005:87

DURING MY FIELDWORK IN BEIJING IN 2007, my son, Benjamin, who was then one and a half years old, attended a local preschool or play group called Color Baby once a week. Chinese parents and the state are keen to develop the kinds of subjectivities that are thought to best guide the country's transition to an innovative society. As a result, preschools have become widespread in the post-Mao era. Beijing and other Chinese cities have thousands of them, and many parents take their child to extracurricular activities such as English lessons, piano, mathematics, and calligraphy in order to ensure that the child develops his or her full potential. This particular preschool was inspired by the American Montessori program,[1] one of many options for Chinese parents and indicative of how childrearing practices have become a battleground for the kind of citizens desired.

Color Baby was located in a park that was particularly crowded in the morning. Toddlers in neat, clean clothes went out for walks with their parents or grandparents, trying out new prams, bicycles, and electrical cars. The park had a copy of an Italian Renaissance garden, complete with classical statues and figures taken from Greek mythology; a children's amusement park with merry-go-rounds, trampolines, and loud electrical toys; and areas in which older people gathered to dance waltzes, sing Chinese opera in the Chinese pagoda, or do tai chi under the weeping willows. Except for the newlywed couples who came in great numbers to be photographed in the French rose garden, this, like most parks in Beijing, was populated mostly by children and old people out to play (*wan*). There was a lake in the middle of the park, filled with pink lotus flowers in summer and covered with ice during the winter. Color Baby was located by the lake, opposite two gigantic revolutionary sculptures of Mao-era athletic-looking youths gazing triumphantly toward the horizon.

At Color Baby, a group of ten children, accompanied by a parent, grandparent, or *ayi* ("nanny," literally "aunt"), met to do oral and physical exercises intended to further their overall development. I experienced great curiosity in regard to my son and the approach to child-raising abroad (*wai guo*), an expression used to refer to the United States or Europe, which were allegedly more developed than China and often conflated in people's imagination. The exercises at Color Baby often involved standing patiently in line, awaiting one's turn, which my son was not accustomed to, which led parents and teachers to comment that he was mischievous (*tiaoqi*). Some parents or grandparents concluded that foreign children were typically independent and confident. While I had the feeling that I was on the verge of losing face when my son refused to stand still or take part in some activities, more pertinent was a sense that mischievousness (*tiaoqi*) indicated brightness (*congming*). When, after the first term, we decided not to continue attending lessons, the teachers offered to give us lessons for free. Having a foreign child in the play group clearly inspired curiosity and was seen as beneficial to the group.

Dressed in colorful uniforms, teachers led the toddlers in rhymes and repeatedly enacted conversations in which there was only one correct way of responding. For example, each of the children was given a colorful balloon. The teachers then went from child to child with a needle to pop the balloons. The children who cried from the bang, either surprised by the loudness of it or disappointed that the balloon they had just been given had been destroyed, were comforted and told to be brave (*yonggan*). Even though the intention was that the children should learn in a "colorful" way, the whole environment was tightly controlled by the teachers. When Benjamin's balloon was popped, he started to cry, and when one of the teachers told him, "Don't cry, little children should be brave!" I reacted emotionally, telling her that Benjamin was in fact very brave. My reaction must have appeared absurd in the eyes of the other teachers and parents, but they accepted my strange behavior without blinking.[2]

This incident later brought to mind the paradigmatic example of mastery play in Freud's *Beyond the Pleasure Principle*, a passage in which Freud describes how a one-and-a-half-year-old child would manipulate objects in order to gain a sense of "mastery" over his mother's going away and returning (Freud 1957:18,

14–16). Throwing a toy out of his cot and declaring it gone (*fort*), then reeling it back and joyfully exclaiming, "There" (*Da*), the child successfully objectified and mastered his emotional distress. The child's mastery of his emotions ties in with Winnicott's account of a boy playing with string as a way of toying with and thereby regaining mastery of his confusing relationship with his mother (Winnicott 1964 [1991]:18–23).

My experience of taking Benjamin to Color Baby, together with the popping of the balloons, has stayed in my mind, tempting me to liken these children to Pavlovian dogs being subjected to operant conditioning. However, some of the parents later explained the exercise in relation to their fear of spoiling their child. In China there is widespread concern that only children may become spoiled and that this will have a negative influence on the child's psychology, making him or her passive, dependent, unfilial, and demanding. In a 1983 article, Ye Gongshao, an educator and specialist in child development, warned that a defining characteristic of families with "little emperors" (*xiao huangdi*) or "little empresses" (*xiao huanhou*) is the four-two-one syndrome (*si-er-yi zonghe-zheng*), i.e., a situation in which two parents and four grandparents pamper just one child (Jing 2000:2). This preoccupation with the dangers of spoiling (*ni ai*, which can be translated as "drowning a child with love"), has increased dramatically since the introduction of the one-child policy, and it forms part of the "education for quality" policy, the aim of which is to create precocious and independent children who are creative and skillful yet also respectful of authorities.[3]

The popping of the balloons can perhaps be understood in relation to a notion of sacrifice, and the assumption that there is more to be gained from self-sacrifice and self-denial than from instant gratification. It is likely that the teachers at Color Baby were preparing the children for the disappointments they would probably face in a competitive and unpredictable future. Instead of drowning children with love, the teachers wanted to prepare them for the painful separations, disappointments, and setbacks of life. Their intention was to teach the children that not everything lies within their grasp. Balloons pop, just as dreams burst. The incident with the balloons reveals the authoritarian way in which *suzhi jiaoyu* is enforced, as well as the double binds that parents and teachers experience when they want to cultivate precocious children who develop an independent self and just as fervently want to raise disciplined children who are respectful of authorities.

The Popular Experts

Chinese educators and parents alike have looked to the West for parental guidance books to identify the qualities that are viewed as lacking among Chinese children and youth. The two popular child-rearing books *Harvard Girl Liu Yiting* by Liu Weihua and Zhang Xinwu, and *Education for Quality in the U.S.* by Huang Quanyu, remind one of the shift from "test-based education" to "education for quality." However, both books have the same aim: to educate one's children in a way that will qualify them for admission to Harvard.

Harvard Girl Liu Yiting became a best seller in 1991 and has been the object of substantial anthropological attention (Kipnis 2006; Woronov 2007; Kuan 2008). It describes the steps a mother took to raise her daughter "scientifically" in order for her to become the first Chinese student to be accepted as a full-fellowship undergraduate at Harvard University. The front cover of the book shows Liu Yiting proudly presenting her admission letter to Harvard. The premise of the book is that any child, if raised properly, can enter Harvard. Harvard is fetishized as the best possible confirmation of a child's quality, as well as the ultimate destination for transnational upward mobility. Liu Yiting's achievement is seen as the outcome of her mother's detailed educational plans, which she began to implement even before her daughter was born (Woronov 2007:44).[4]

In 2001 another child-rearing book, *Education for Quality in the U.S.*, by Huang Quanyu, became a best seller. Like Liu Yiting, Huang Quanyu is also well known in Beijing. The book is written from the perspective of a father raising his son in the United States and seeking to identify American child-rearing practices that enhance the "quality" (*suzhi*) of a child and make him or her a potential millionaire or winner of a Nobel Prize (Woronov 2007:41–42). Huang Quanyu argues that the American educational system encourages individual development and nurtures each student's "genuine self." As a result, American children are "self-actualized," as opposed to Chinese children, who merely learn to comport themselves according to certain "social roles." American children do more than learn facts by rote; they acquire flexible skills in meeting the challenge of a wide range of intellectual tasks. This gives them the confidence to take risks and to develop entrepreneurial skills. According to Woronov, by the year 2000 "the values of self-discipline and self-sacrifice seem old-fashioned to many well-off urban Chinese parents, who increasingly identify with the values of the bourgeois West: self-actualization, creative self-expression and instant gratification through consumption."

Teresa Kuan's description of an evening course on parenting skills that she attended in 2004 in the city of Kunming, Yunnan province, is thought-provoking. One lesson was on the theme of mother love, and the message was that "'excessive love' or spoiling (*ni ai*) could be harmful to the child" (Kuan 2008:xii–xv). The teacher told an exemplary story about two parents who drove their thirteen-year-old son out to a remote village. They told him to find a meal on his own, and then abandoned him. The teacher insisted to her class that these parents really did love their son. In fact, they were tremendously worried that their son had no sense of self, that he was too introverted and stifled (*yayi*). They worried that the junior school he was going to attend the following semester would only intensify these traits, given the large numbers of students in each class. This lesson in self-sufficiency, the teacher claimed, actually helped him. This was an example of a kind of love that, as the teacher explained, was scientifically proven to be beneficial rather than harmful to a child's development (Kuan 2008:xii–xv). Coddling and helping a child with his or her tasks may, in this view, be spurious forms of maternal love, and "unscientific." Indeed, they may actually lead to "mother harm" (*mu hai*). The kind of love that comes naturally (*jianglin zai ni tou shang*, literally "falls on your head") may inhibit a child's development. From this teacher's point of view, proper love is the kind of love that encourages rather than inhibits a child's ability to act independently. Here, the teacher echoes a common Chinese concern that children are too dependent and introverted, by contrast with American children, who are taught to take the initiative and to be self-confident. As Kuan points out, in the case above it is hard to escape the irony that the child could become independent only if the parents took the initiative, determining the rules of the game, driving their son out to a remote place and instructing him to find a meal on his own. This case seems to confirm Andrew Kipnis's point that *suzhi* discourse is far from neoliberal but rather is enforced in an authoritarian way.

This example, whereby parents abandon their child in a remote village to foster his development of self-sufficiency, would undoubtedly be seen as extreme by most parents in China. It uncannily brings to mind the story of Hansel and Gretel, who are abandoned by their parents in the woods. Even though such parental actions may seem pathological, the challenge is to understand what underlies parental anxieties about cultivating a quality child who will be successful in tomorrow's world. To some extent parental anxieties reflect a contradiction between an idealized Western perspective and a more traditionally

Chinese perspective on how to manage uncertainty in an increasingly competitive and crowded society. The one-child policy only exacerbates this tension because, while discipline is encouraged, the pressures of creating and educating a perfect only child are enormous.

The illustration above reveals a widespread concern about only children who are dependent, introverted, and passive. In responding to this concern by sacrificing maternal love and asserting harsh discipline, parents may make matters worse. Once, when my son tripped but got up by himself, an old woman who assumed that I did not understand Chinese, commented, "The mother does not even help him get up!" A young man, who was an official in the Chinese army, promptly corrected her by saying that foreign children are "tough" (*li hai*) or "brave" (*young gan*), whereas Chinese children are more dependent and more easily given to crying when they encounter minor obstacles and disappointments. "Look at him, he's doing fine! He has already forgotten that he fell down." "Does he eat by himself?" people would ask me. Some seemed to feel that Benjamin's early independence implied a sacrifice of parental love.

Talking to parents and grandparents in the neighborhood where I lived provided insight into the dilemmas and contradictions (*maodun*) that parents face in raising children. One mother put it this way:

Chinese society is so competitive, so like every Chinese parent I want to give my child the best start in life. But I try not to spoil my child too much. She is all I have got. I think a child's development is many things. It is not only learning to walk and to talk. It also has to do with creative skills, such as music, dancing, painting, and social skills. These things are important for children's development. In the past they were overlooked. It is important for children to learn from others, to develop their social skills. I care for you [*guan xin*] so you must also care for me. It is harmful to put too much pressure on children, but spoiling is also a problem. They should be given the time to play [*wan*], but up to a certain limit. What happens when a child starts school? If a child has been spoiled, always having his or her way, never having to bear failure [*chengshou shibai*], how can that child cope when starting schooling?

What is at stake here seems to be an anxiety related to raising a single child who will be so superior and special that he or she will readily find a place in China's competitive market economy. In contemporary China, both China's own cultural traditions and ideas borrowed from the West are fraught with ambiguity. Parents simultaneously wish to develop a child's potential so that he or she becomes "self-actualized" and independent, just as American children are imagined to be. At the same time, parents experience a desire to cultivate strong feelings of attachment, love, and loyalty between themselves and their children. A child must be disciplined enough to be successful within a competitive educational system *and* to remain filial to his or her parents and able to take care of them in the future. Similar double binds have followed from the "education for quality" reforms in the tertiary sector.

Suzhi jiaoyu within Higher Education

In describing his efforts to address China's urgent need for a talented elite of innovators, former vice premier Li Lanqing declared, "Students are buried in an endless flood of homework and sit for one mock entrance exam after another, leaving them with heads swimming and eyes blurred" (Hulbert 2007:3). Since the 1980s the Chinese educational system's reputed prioritizing of rote memorization over creativity and critical thinking has been, and continues to be, a topic of intense debate. *Suzhi jiaoyu* involved an attempt to reform the educational system so that it produced innovative citizens able to compete in a global knowledge economy, rather than "test machines" who learned for the purpose of passing exams.

The term *suzhi jiaoyu* emerged during the 1980s, and in 1985 the Central Committee of the Communist Party stated that "raising the suzhi of the people of the nation was the basic goal of education system reform" (Hulbert 2007:298). *Suzhi jiaoyu* is best translated as "education for quality," since it is not the quality of the educational system that is at stake so much as its ability to improve the quality of the people (Kipnis 2006:301). The policy of *suzhi jiaoyu* came as a reaction to test-based education (*ying shi jiaoyu*), and was inspired by the American notion of "competence education" as well as other, somewhat contradictory ideas derived from foreign models of child-rearing and education. Moreover, the call for *suzhi jiaoyu* can be seen as part of an attempt to revitalize the strength of the nation, and is tied to a tale said to originate during the Opium Wars (1839–1842 and 1856–1860), which left China weakened and impoverished as "the sick man of Asia."

Dewey as a "Second Confucius"

The last imperial regime collapsed in 1911, and in the period that followed, several European countries tried to colonize China by military means. Anti-Japanese and anti-European power movements spread throughout China (Qi 2008:257). At the same time, some Chinese intellectuals advocated learning Western philosophy and theories, especially those from America. Among the Western theories translated into Chinese and prominently acknowledged by Chinese intellectuals were John Dewey's theories of social science and education.[5] In fact, Dewey achieved such high status that he was awarded the "Second Confucius" prize by the University of China in 1920, though as the historian Qi Jie points out, the word "Confucius" in this context does not mean that Dewey's thoughts were similar to those of Confucius; rather that he was a thinker as great as Confucius. I think this highlights an attempt to reconcile two seemingly incompatible phenomena: the hierarchical ideology of Confucianism and the egalitarian ideology of John Dewey.

Chinese intellectuals integrated Dewey's pragmatism and Marxism in what became "the May Fourth Movement." The movement appealed for social, political, and educational reform (Qi 2008:257–260). According to Stig Thøgersen, this resulted in the promulgation of a new set of pedagogical practices, known as the 1922 school system, that is strikingly similar to contemporary American practices (Thøgersen 2002:61). New curriculum guidelines followed in 1923, and lessons were now carried out in the modern vernacular language, which replaced classical Chinese in all textbooks. This was a significant departure from the previous educational pattern of mimetically learning to recite the Confucian classics.

Under the Confucian system, education was intended to prepare children for the civil servant examination (ke ju zhi). The higher the score, the better one's position in the civil service. One of Confucius's well-known proverbs reads, "Studying is for the purpose of becoming a civil servant." It was a virtue to be obedient to one's superior. The notions of Dewey's democracy and science enabled Chinese intellectuals to rethink the character of social relationships, including the relationships between students and teachers and a language reform.[6]

In the 1920s, Dewey's pragmatism had been used as an inspiration for carrying out a school reform in which "child-centred education" was the goal (Qi 2008:268). Dewey's critique of traditional notions of the child as a passive receptor of external data was adopted by Chinese educational reformers who, following Dewey, saw a need for a new approach to education in order to create innovative individuals and useful knowledge.

According to Dewey, society depends upon imaginative and creative individuals. Therefore, an education process must reflect the desires and interests of the pupil (Dewey 1964:xxvi–xxviii). The relationship between teacher and pupil is reciprocal, in the sense that the teacher is not an authority who dispenses ideas to be absorbed by the pupil but rather a catalyst in enabling the child to develop his or her own ideas. In this way, the school is "child-centred." Qi has pointed out that whereas Dewey's project of education was to create knowledge and skills that are of use in society, education for the new Chinese intellectuals was combined with a Marxist project and thus had the aim of reforming Chinese society and remolding Chinese life and the Chinese individual (Qi 2008:271). However, when Maoist Marxism was introduced, Dewey's social pragmatism, like the Confucian order, was denounced by the political regime as reactionary and imperialist (Qi 2008:261).

In many ways the discourse of *suzhi jiaoyu*, which has been so influential since the 1980s, appears to reiterate ideas put forward by the New Culture Movement at the beginning of the century. The critique of the Confucian school system, with its prioritization of reciting the classics, now seems to find resonance in the critique of test-based education (*yinghi jiaoyu*) in which the goal of education is passing exams. For twenty years, up to the end of the Mao period, Dewey's thought came under severe criticism. Since the 1980s, however, Dewey's thought has been read by a "second generation of new Chinese intellectuals" (Qi 2008:273) in the light of *suzhi* policies and terminology.

The democratic ideas that are tightly bound up with Dewey's philosophy of education, whereby the teacher's main role is "the liberation of the student" (Qi 2008:xxviii), are, however, not entirely compatible with the Chinese authoritarian form of government. As a result, educational reformers have formulated their ideas for educational reform within the language of the party, with its rhetoric of improving the quality of the population, as well as seeking to create the skills needed in a global knowledge society. This may in part explain why *suzhi jiaoyu* is experienced as highly contradictory when put in practice.

I will now place this rather abstract discussion on firmer ground by turning to the ways in which my interlocutors reflected on the *suzhi jiaoyu* reforms.

Ideals and Practice

Parents, teachers, and young people all consider that "education for quality" would be well nigh impossible to put into practice unless the whole educational system were changed. Practically everyone I spoke to pointed out the contradiction that despite the government's call for creativity and an end to rote memorization, the higher education system is still based on an exam system whose rationale is a student's ability to memorize. One student invoked the reality that higher education involves a competitive struggle for a scarce resource with the remark "It's just a name—*suzhi jiaoyu* can only work in the West, where there are fewer people and less competition."

What then, is *suzhi jiaoyu* in practice?

Suzhi jiaoyu covers a broad range of changes in curricula, including the addition of color to textbooks and the introduction of supplementary courses (Hulbert 2007). In practice, *suzhi jioayu* means that students have to take a certain number of extracurricular courses focused on artistic qualifications, sports, social work, military training, psychological development, and the like—courses meant to ensure a student's all-round development. These courses are not graded, and often students do not have the surplus time and energy for them. Students may not take these courses—like the ideological course on Marxism described earlier, for example—very seriously. Quite often they are regarded as a waste, because they take time away from courses that must be passed to reach the next level and thereby obtain a high GPA. Furthermore, there is an authoritarian element in the way in which these extracurricular activities are implemented, since students are denied any choice in how they spend their "leisure time."[7]

Gu Wei explained the meaning of *suzhi jiaoyu* in this way: "It is all about developing yourself, the quality . . . maybe you don't have it, but it is something that can be developed . . . like the ability to communicate with others and to lead others, to have self-confidence and to be able to take risks." Like many students, Gu Wei emphasized that there was a relatively better environment at Tsinghua University and Beijing University for "all-round development." Referring to the availability of extracurricular activities, he added:

But still you cannot escape the fact that there are many exams. Let me put it this way. Take, for instance, Harvard University. When students graduate from Harvard they know that they can find a good job, so they can focus more on personal development (*ziwo fazhan*). In America, students have a supervisor, someone responsible for the well-being of students, not only their academic achievement. At Tsinghua we have one also, but whenever students contact their supervisor, he or she will be too busy. In reality you are alone. There is nowhere to get help. It's like . . . it's just a name . . . it's like China wants to have a great educational system, like in America, but the reality we Chinese students face is different.

In his work on life stages, the social psychologist Erik Erikson described the period of youth as a "psychosocial moratorium," during which a young adult "through free role experimentation may find a niche in some section of his society, a niche which is firmly defined and yet seems to be uniquely made for him" (Erikson [1968] 1994:156). "Moratorium" here refers to a period in which adult commitments are delayed. "It is a period that is characterized by a selective permissiveness on the part of society and of provocative playfulness on the part of youth" (Erikson [1968] 1994:156).

According to Yunxiang Yan, a "youth culture" has emerged in rural China, marked by a strong desire to pursue personal happiness in the form of material comforts, play, romance, and better jobs. These aspirations are challenging the previously dominant Communist ideology that denies individual interests and promotes asceticism (Yan 1999:81). In my experience, however, students at both Tsinghua University and Beijing University often described their everyday lives as being in a routine, following a monotonous movement from dormitory, to canteen, to classroom, to canteen, to classroom, to library, to canteen, to dormitory. This pattern echoes descriptions of one's life course as endless study, moving from the best primary schools, to the best secondary schools, to the best high schools, and finally to a top university. Students described their youth as a time of necessary self-sacrifice; their present suffering is tied to a promise of future gratification. At the same time, many people long for a more "colorful life," with a greater sense of self-determination and self-realization. Students invoke a sense that there is more to life than studying and that a person's quality depends on more than merely his or her GPA.

One student put it this way: "We use mostly American textbooks, but this does not mean that the educational systems are alike. Even though everybody feels that the Chinese educational system is full of flaws, it is hard to make any real changes. We are too many people . . . So what can you do? The competition is so fierce, because everybody is afraid of not being excellent enough . . . not making it to the top."

This focus on diligence and self-sacrifice is all the more pronounced at elite universities such as Beijing and Tsinghua, where the level of ambition is higher than at other schools. People are conscious of the fact that they are competing against students who have the highest GPAs in China as a whole. Furthermore, these elite students are probably more diligent and hardworking than the average Chinese college student. Student workloads also depend on the major the student chooses. Natural science students have more classes, as well as having to do exercises in laboratories. Students of the humanities and social sciences generally have more spare time and tend to describe their lives as more "colorful." However, while there are great differences between students and their parents that reflect their social backgrounds, most students, in my experience, see self-discipline as a prerequisite to, but not a guarantee of, educational success.

A Back Door to Corruption

Some students, especially those from less-privileged or rural backgrounds, are critical of the notion of *suzhi jiaoyu*, regarding it as a back door to corruption. Typical of the remarks of rural students were those of Bai Gang:

There are fewer students like us [i.e., rural students] by the year. Test-based education has its problems, but at least it is fair. *Suzhi jiaoyu* is difficult to put into practice. Sometimes a talent is invented if people have money and the right connections. *Suzhi jiaoyu* is for those who can afford it, those who have something to fall back on, whose parents can arrange a space for them at a top university or even pay for a scholarship so that they can go abroad.

Referring to her fieldwork in rural Jiangxi province, Rachel Murphy makes the very poignant observation that "internalizing and resisting [*suzhi jiaoyu*] are not mutually exclusive, and most people's responses incorporate elements of both" (Murphy 2004:14). This is also true of university students.

As we will recall from Chapter 4, a friend of Bai's had been granted a Ph.D. position because his father had contacts within the party, whereas Bai was struggling to find work, even though his grades were better than those of his friend. Andrew Kipnis's work provides evidence of this discrimination. Special schools are reserved for training and providing credentials for party members and, in some elite cases, their children. Neither the process of admission to these schools nor their training programs are open to public evaluation, though the nation is assured that all graduates have achieved the highest levels of *suzhi* (Kipnis 2007:388).

Suzhi jiaoyu policy means that only a few people, believed to have a special talent, are able to enter university without taking the dreaded college entrance exams. For instance, winners of the national physics competition or the national English competition, or people who have some unique talent such as being able to play a musical instrument, can in special cases be granted a scholarship on different terms. In this way, *suzhi jiaoyu* is tied to a system of selecting a few exceptionally talented persons (*ren cai*). This was the case for Ryan.

A Model Student

Ryan, a sensitive and confident nineteen-year-old from Nanjing, explained that he had entered Tsinghua without taking the ordinary college entrance examination because he had won the national physics competition while in high school. His English was excellent, as he had been in the United States for a year during the eighth grade, accompanying his father, a professor in one of the natural sciences. Even though he explained that he had taken another kind of test, which in his view required more independent thinking, he was struggling to find out what he wanted to do in life. Furthermore, in his experience, being a model student caused considerable ambiguity, as he felt he was not essentially any different from other students, even though people from his old high school considered him to be a genius. He described this awkwardness whenever he returned home, saying, "People treat me as if I was a famous person."[8] "What they don't know is that there are so many '*da niu*' [literally "big cows," usually translated as "monsters"] at Tsinghua!" The term "monster" is a slang expression for unusually "brainy" individuals, and it is most often used to describe people who have a talent for natural science subjects. His comment is reminiscent of Susan Greenhalgh's description of some of the birth-planning cadres, in the initial stages of the implementation of the one-child policy, who were given awards for being "model workers," sacrificing their own families for the sake of the nation (Greenhalgh 2005). It seems that the model citizens of today embody the greatness of the nation through their *individual* talents rather than through their sacrifice for the common good. Janne Breinegaard has described a similar phenomenon in Japan, where Japanese students who have studied abroad and returned to Japan are accorded special status (Breinegaard 2005).

Ryan's experience of living abroad led him to reflect on the different approaches to education in China and the United States, including the relationships among teachers, parents, and students. For instance, he compared the way people are seated in classrooms in these two countries: "In China, people have a fixed seat, and parents put pressure on the teacher to give their child a good space at the front to ensure that they have the best possibilities for hearing the teacher and a good view to the blackboard." In the United States, he recalled, students and teachers determined seating arrangements, and parents had no say in the matter. He therefore considered American students to be more independent of their parents, since they had a direct relationship with their teacher.

Even though Ryan highlighted what he saw as the qualities of the American educational system, he described himself as being "essentially no different" from other Chinese students who had been accepted on the basis of "test-based education." His parents had chosen his major, electrical engineering, since it was a "hot topic," though he did not really know what he was interested in. He asked me whether it was true that people in the West tend to choose their majors according to their interests and not according to their prospects of obtaining a job with a high salary. Being abroad had made him reflect on the way he had been "educated within materialism, and brought up to believe that there is no God." He said that he struggled to find the meaning of life, and had started "believing in God, not the party."

Ryan was extremely critical of the Chinese educational system. "It has so many faults, it is almost a failure," he said. He was referring to the endless competition, obliging most people, including himself, to "follow the trend" of studying more or less constantly in order to obtain good exam results. "It has become a habit to be excellent," he said. And while he found this position depressing and morally dubious, he also said he found it hard to escape.

A few months later Ryan sent me an e-mail message in which he wanted to introduce me to his new girlfriend. He wrote that he now realized that "the meaning of life is love."

A Teacher's Dilemma

One day as Jia Ling and I walked by the frozen lakes to the east of the Tsinghua University campus, she spoke of her students. "They are in a place where so many others wished they could be, but they are not happy!" As a teacher she disliked having to grade students, knowing that "every time there is an exam someone will be at the bottom, and it is as if this person has no worth as a human being." At the same time, Jia said, sometimes the students who got high marks were in fact lacking in other ways. She invoked the famous phrase by Lu Xun,[9] "the child is half dead," referring to the arduous task of memorizing thousands of Chinese characters and repeating Confucian sayings.

In the same way, she explained, there was something missing in the personality of many of her students. They might have a high GPA, but they were introverted and lacking in "social skills": "My students do not spend much time playing. They face a lot of pressure, having to memorize a lot of facts in order to reproduce this knowledge in exams. Unlike students in the West, they rarely have girlfriends and boyfriends, they do not drink, they don't go out, but what they do is play computer games. They try to escape from reality and to forget the pressure by losing themselves on the Net." It was clearly a common view among students that time spent playing was time lost for studying.

Jia Ling compared the difference between test-based (*yingshi jiaoyu*) learning and education for quality (*suzhi jiaoyu*) with the difference between knowing and mastering a language—a difference between being "like a dictionary" and being able to use language creatively in social contexts. She thought that students might benefit more from practicing oral English with one another, rather than through individual cramming for exams or walking around campus reciting words to themselves, which was not uncommon. She also tried to devote time to classroom discussion, though she felt that the call for *suzhi jiaoyu* created a dilemma, since spending time on extracurricular material could too easily mean time lost on material necessary for exam purposes. Jia Ling herself was in a quandary about how to reconcile these pedagogical aims.

Teachers like Jia Ling are evaluated in terms of their students' exam results, as well as, in some cases, their students' views of the teacher, exemplifying a *suzhi jiaoyu* approach.[10] Jia Ling explained that she tried to find a balance, and did in fact allow her students to use the English language to talk about things that were meaningful to them, such as love relationships, relationships with their parents, their future, and so on. It seemed to her that while the strongest of her students might benefit from such an approach, the weaker students might easily fall behind.

In other words, the new ethos of a more student-driven environment based on creative experimentation and dialogue is at odds with the competitive character of the Chinese educational system, where exams based on memorization are an inescapable part of reaching the next level. Furthermore, there are practical constraints, such as the large class sizes, that make it difficult to implement the promotion of student dialogue. Despite the official position that dialogue should be encouraged between teachers and students, people in Zouping county, where Stig Thøgersen carried out fieldwork, described education as a situation in which teachers talk and students listen. He argues that any reform that involves students' speaking more, even without being asked, can probably succeed only if it goes hand in hand with a democratization of the political system (Thøgersen 2002:247). According to students and teachers at Tsinghua and Beijing universities, teachers do most of the talking and students listen. Jia Ling's students pointed out that she was an unusual teacher and that, except for the many laboratory exercises that natural science students have to undertake, in most classes the teachers lecture and the students take notes. Furthermore, as Jia Ling's reflections in Chapter 3 revealed, not only are students limited in terms of what kinds of questions they can ask, but teachers have to be cautious and stay within the boundaries of what is socially and politically acceptable.

One day, when Jia Ling visited me, she noticed that I had Gao Xingjian's novel *One Man's Bible* lying beside my bed, a book that she had heard about but not read. She said she felt that Gao Xingjian had probably been given the Nobel Prize because of his critical account of China and of the Cultural Revolution. "A Western audience likes that." However, she also found it sad that the Chinese state had not recognized the achievement, even though Gao Xingjian was an émigré and had become a French citizen. In this connection, Jia Ling pointed to the irony, which had not escaped many students, that *suzhi jiaoyu* was promoted both on the grounds that it was necessary to reduce pressure on young people and on the grounds that China has not yet had a legitimate Chinese Nobel prizewinner.

Tea Pavilion

When I returned to Beijing in July 2012, I was eager to meet Jia Ling again. Much had happened in her life since I had last seen her. I knew from our e-mail correspondence that she had received her Ph.D. in Chinese literature at Cambridge University in the United Kingdom and that she had returned to China to teach English at Tsinghua. I was curious to understand what had brought her back to China.

When I approached the West Gate, I was surprised to find an enormous crowd of people lined up in front of it. Jia Ling called me on my cell phone and said that she would come out to let me in so that we could skip the line. Once we were inside the gate, she explained that these people were tourists—mostly parents with their child, who hoped to realize a family dream by one day entering one of China's top universities. It reminded me of a queue I had seen about a year earlier in front of the John Harvard statue at Harvard University. A busload of mostly Chinese tourists were clustered around the statue, taking photos. At Tsinghua, Jia Ling echoed the thought I had had in Harvard Yard: "So few of them are going to make it." Jia Ling talked about how her oldest sister's daughter had just finished the college entrance examination (*gaokao*) and despite the fact that she had spent a year of studying, largely deprived of play and leisure, she had not made it into a top university. "My sister is really crushed," she said. "What about her daughter?" I asked. "She is disappointed, too," Jia Ling said. "But she does not really like to study. She wants to have fun, and now my sister wants to take her to Disneyland in Hong Kong." Jia Ling sounded disappointed and explained that she thought her niece could experience much more by coming to Beijing.

We shared some steaming-hot dumplings and chrysanthemum tea at a restaurant where we had often had lunch together in the past, and she told me about another tragic case of suicide and how the university had covered it up. This brought us to the subject of *suzhi jiaoyu*. "This is still a hot topic," Jia Ling said, and went on to tell me that she had recently been at a teachers' retreat with her department. The aim was to talk about improving the quality of teaching. "This was such a weird experience," she said. The retreat had taken place at a special resort adjoining the Summer Palace. It had turned out that this place was owned by the Chinese Communist Party and was used by party officials to hold meetings. "This was the most beautiful place," Jia Ling said. "Just like the Summer Palace, with a beautiful lake and traditional Chinese architecture." Jia Ling explained that her head of department had suggested they have a meeting in a particular tea pavilion that one reached via an arched bridge that had a stunning view of the lake. Once the group had been seated, a waitress showed up. "She was extraordinarily beautiful and dressed in a silk *qi pao* [a traditional Chinese dress]," Jia Ling said. The waitress told them that this place was only for people having lunch. The head of department was reluctant to accept this and asked whether his group could order a pot of tea and sit there while having a meeting. After some negotiation the waitress confessed that she had to keep the place prepared for whenever a group of party officials might turn up for lunch. Somewhat dispirited, the group had to withdraw to a restaurant outside the precinct.

The group's conversation turned to the issue of party membership, for everyone had assumed that they were all party members for more or less pragmatic reasons. But when Jia Ling boldly declared, "I am not a member of the party," the head of department broke the awkward silence that followed, saying, "No, but Jia Ling is a very dedicated person with a strong personal integrity." Jia Ling said that she was warmed by this comment but also provoked by the assumption that there was a connection between personal morality and party membership. She responded by saying, "In fact I do not think there is any connection between being a party member and being a person of high moral standing." "How did they respond?" I asked, somewhat surprised by her confrontational attitude. "I think they agreed," she said. "Some of them nodded."

After this seminar she was a little afraid that she had jeopardized her relationship to her boss. In fact, the very opposite was true, for a few weeks later he had called her to his office and asked if she would accept the highly prestigious task of proofreading the English translation of the memoirs of a highly placed former member of the government. Jia Ling's boss explained that his department had been entrusted with this task and that he felt she would be the most suitable person for the job. She could not say no to this assignment, though it would be extraordinarily time-consuming and the honorarium was a mere token. Reading these memoirs, Jia Ling was nonetheless surprised by evidence of the government's determination to reform the educational system. "In fact they know about the real problems. They just don't know how to make the changes," she said.

When I asked her why she thought that she had been selected for this assignment, Jia Ling responded that it had everything to do with her Cambridge Ph.D. "There is a lot of prestige associated with this. Therefore I can get away with some diversion from the norm. I think this makes me a little bit mysterious and I don't mind being mysterious. In fact, I would like to retain a little bit of that sense of mystery so that I can continue to be left alone."

Imagining America

When Tang Meiji, a student from Shanghai, was admitted to Harvard, she was portrayed as every parent's dream child. A media frenzy followed. "What does her success tell us?" asked a headline for an article in the *Shanghai Students' Post* (Hulbert 2007:1–3). According to an article in the *New York Times*, Tang Meiji herself responded very ambiguously to being represented as a success story that Chinese parents and educators were eager to emulate. "Please don't call me Harvard girl," she told many magazine interviewers, and she referred to Liu Yiting, a student six years ahead of her who became a national celebrity in 1999, when she became the first Chinese undergraduate to receive a full scholarship to Harvard.

As soon as Tang Meiji entered Harvard, she "discovered what she would really like to do." Her dream was to make liberal education's goal of well-roundedness and self-fulfillment "more real in China" (Hulbert 2007:1–3). In her experience, America had come to stand for "a less pressured and more fulfilling form of education." "There is something in the American educational system that helps America hold its position in the world," she told Ann Hulbert, a journalist from the *New York Times*. However, the Chinese media continued to portray her as an exceptional talent who, despite a GPA that was not even in the top 10 percent, excelled in certain subjects and had won more than seventy-six prizes at the "city level" or above (Hulbert 2007:1–3). She came to embody the ideas of *suzhi jiaoyu* that had informed Chinese debates about education since the 1980s, but she also exemplified the very competitiveness that the *suzhi jiaoyu* reforms were intended to curb.

Like Tang Meiji, Liu Xing received admission letters from two American universities in the summer of 2006. Although she had read books that *she* liked, had found time to spend with her boyfriend and other friends, and had extracurricular interests, she had managed to achieve what so many were unable to. It is difficult to say to what extent this reflected her personality and perseverance, but I think it is important to note her upbringing in an educated home that encouraged self-confidence and reading whatever most interested her.

Liu Xing was quite passionate on the subject of *suzhi jioayu*, which she felt should be expanded to include more than a small elite that had received full emotional and economic support from its parents and therefore had been able to succeed in life without "desperate cramming for exams." "This is such a limited view of success," Liu Xing said. "Striving to be the top, only for the sake of being the top, it's depressing." She felt that more vocational schools were needed. Her own success, however, had been achieved unequivocally, as she was among the lucky few who had received admission to a Ph.D. program at an American university. Liu Xing said she wanted to do a Ph.D. in law at an American university because she wanted to learn more about the world and meet other people. She also thought the American educational system was more focused on critical thinking than the Chinese one.

One day Liu Xing and I discussed the American independent movie *Little Miss Sunshine*, which both of us had seen. This comedy centers on how members of an American family struggle for success in the eyes of others. In the film, the father of the family puts pressure on his son, out of fear that he will become a "loser." Consequently, the boy stops talking. The movie also portrays his little sister's comical attempts to win a beauty pageant called Little Miss Sunshine, despite her rather homely looks. Liu Xing found the film to be funny, but she said that she was surprised to find that American society was so competitive.

In her analysis of Chinese parents' fascination with American educational practices, Terry Woronov sees *suzhi jiaoyu* as a form of Occidentalism, arguing that it is focused on the category of "education for quality" that has more meaning for his (Chinese) readers than his (American) informants. Woronov argues that Huang Quanyu's parental guidance book, *Education for Quality in the U.S.*, ignores class, race, and region, and makes a school in a wealthy Cincinnati area representative of American culture per se. Chinese readers fail to appreciate that the book is biased toward a particular class perspective, and they are therefore incredulous when they learn that the American educational system has its flaws and problems, including unequal educational funding, standards, and opportunities, as well as school violence. Accordingly, the understandings of Chinese parents with regard to American educational practices are "not derived from the reality of what the West offers, but like Occidentalism in general are a self-contained, self-referential reality, the terms of which are determined in local standards" (Woronov 2007:47).

In practice, however, the notion of Occidentalism does not really capture what was at stake for either Wu Jiao or Liu Xing. In fact it makes more sense to say that they were, in their different ways, simultaneously critical of their own societies and of the West. As we recall, Liu Xing did not want her children to grow up to become bananas. She simultaneously wanted to hold on to her cultural roots, or a disposition for filiality, *and* to seek new opportunities for self-realization and cosmopolitanism abroad.

"Life Could Be More Colorful"

According to Wu Jiao, a student of electrical engineering at Tsinghua, *suzhi jiaoyu* is impossible to enforce in China. He gave the following example: "If I had been the top fourth in my province, I could have chosen my major. But I was only the top fifth. . . . Actually my father chose my major and asked me if it was all right. The first thing we considered was the job opportunities, the salary, the money."

What Wu Jiao is referring to here is the tricky college admission procedure, whereby a student, or his or her family, has to apply for admission before actually knowing the result of his or her college entrance examination. "We took a

chance when choosing my major," Wu Jiao said. His father had listed automation science as a first priority, since he considered this a "hot topic." Electrical
engineering was his second choice. So when Wu Jiao says that he "could have
chosen his major" if he had obtained a higher score, he refers to the connection between grades and actual prospects, and thus the inevitable competition.
In other words, only when one has made it to the top, in the sense of having
achieved the highest possible score on the college entrance exam, is it possible
to choose for oneself or to have one's wishes granted.

Wu Jiao was interested in discussing to what extent people in America and
Europe chose their own majors. I said that in Denmark the majority of students
chose their own majors, but that grades were also important. I mentioned that
in Denmark majors such as psychology, literature, anthropology, and political science required high grades. He was intrigued by this and said, "Denmark
sounds so romantic, like a fairy tale country," undoubtedly alluding to Hans
Christian Andersen's fairy tales, which are well known in China. He explained
that in China the situation was exactly the opposite. Hot subjects such as economics and automation science required high grades because these majors led
to high-paying jobs. As I did not want to create too rosy a picture of Danish society, I explained that in Denmark young people with an arts degree often had
a hard time finding a job after graduation, to which Wu Jiao rightly pointed out
that "many Chinese college students have a hard time finding jobs too."

Vanessa Fong has noted that as the numbers of job seekers with higher education degrees increase, employers raise the bar of minimum educational qualifications. Good jobs became more and more elusive, as diplomas, expectations,
and consumption demands skyrocket (Fong 2004:88). Sometimes employers
look for college degrees even when hiring for menial positions like restaurant
waiters (Kuan 2008:101). Fong points to the irony that though the one-child
policy was designed to alleviate population pressure, it has actually created a
generation of young people whose rising educational levels and desire for elite,
high-paying jobs are outpacing the country's economic development (Kuan
2008:90). Wu Jiao felt that because of the massive competition in the labor market, it was not enough to have a degree. As a result, "people also try to focus on
self-development [*ziwo fazhan*]."

Wu Jiao also confessed to being unsure about what he wanted to do in the
future. He felt he knew little about the world. He had always been interested in
history, but as a historian he felt he would not be able to make enough money

to provide for his family, which could well comprise himself, his wife, one or two children, and his parents. "But even now I am not sure about the choice of major. At times I find it tedious, meaningless. I feel I have lost interest in it. There is no happiness." Sitting in the café among many foreign students, he commented that he felt they had so much more time to go out, to communicate with other people and to do what they were interested in.

In fact people at Tsinghua just follow a trend. It is all about studying, getting high marks, a good job and a high salary. Many people lose their interests, and some even commit suicide. I hate this trend. Even I don't go out much. I have some friends outside campus, and sometimes we meet to have lunch and chat, but not so often. I find that transportation is a waste of time, and afterwards I will feel guilty.

Wu Jiao's reflections revealed a tension between a desire for self-actualization and a coexisting imperative of familial duty. Pursuing a major chosen by his father in order to gain a sufficient income would, he imagined, eventually enable him to fulfil the generational contract, have a family of his own, and continue the family line. In other words, the moral tension between a need for self-sacrifice and a desire for self-actualization must be understood in relation to socioeconomic constraints, as well as the structure of an educational system where being top fifth, not top fourth, makes a difference in terms of the possibility of self-determination.

During the course of talking, listening to foreign music, drinking coffee, and watching people whom Wu Jiao saw as leading lives that were more "colorful" (*you zi wei*—literally "to have taste"—the opposite of being bland), Wu Jiao spoke more and more passionately about becoming a history teacher, and wanting to resist prevailing trends and experience more in life. "I think maybe I have to make a big choice in life." When I asked him what his parents would say, he avoided the question and showed more interest in hearing about the situation "abroad." He talked about an American student at Beijing University who was a friend of his. Wu Jiao referred to this friend as "the boat guy," because he had told Wu Jiao that he had spent some time traveling around the world with a group of friends by boat. Wu Jiao laughed at what he thought was an impossible dream.

We are used to this tradition, to pursue higher education, from the best high schools to the best university, bachelor's degree, a master's and then a Ph.D. and a well-paying job. This is the typical road for parents and even students of Tsinghua. But life could be more colorful. There can be a lot of animals and trees in the jungle, not just one bird or one tree but more diversity, people with different characters who have different opinions. The most important thing for my generation is that we take charge of the world and get involved in the society. It is difficult for us. Change takes time. The society has changed, but the thinking has not changed so much. Maybe in the future our children will be happier. Maybe in the future nobody will tell our children what to do. They should make the choices on their own.

It became clear to me that while Wu Jiao dreamt of a more "colorful" life, he did not find it realistic that his generation could become "involved in society." There was no escaping the trend, he felt, and all one could hope was that life would be better for the next generation.

In my introduction to this book, I cited Wu Jiao's image of being on a train where everybody holds on in order not to fall off—his way of capturing the experience of the pressures and competitiveness of everyday life. He also mentioned that economic progress had led to the construction of a lot of high-rise buildings, yet not much had changed because he felt stuck in a routine of studying a major chosen by his father and longing for a greater degree of self-determination. I was reminded of Walter Benjamin's desolate view of progress:

A Klee painting named "Angulus Novus" shows an angel looking as though he is about to move away from something he is fixedly contemplating. His eyes are staring, his mouth is open, his wings are spread. This is how one pictures the angel of history. His face is turned toward the past. Where we perceive a chain of events, he sees one single catastrophe which keeps piling wreckage upon wreckage and hurls it in front of his feet. The angel would like to stay, awaken the dead, and make whole what has been smashed. But a storm is blowing from Paradise; it has got caught in his wings with such violence that the angel can no longer close them. This storm irresistibly propels him into the future to which his back is turned, while the pile of debris before him grows skyward. This storm is what we call progress. (Walter Benjamin, *Theses on the Philosophy of History*)[11]

Is such a pessimistic view of progress justified? Although people from all walks of life in urban China struggle with the pressures of life, it is also true that everyone feels that life "now" is better than "before." Wu Jiao also mentioned that his grandparents had lived through the Japanese invasion and had survived the Communist Revolution, including the hardships of the Cultural Revolution, when his grandfather was stigmatized as a "black element." During the great drought and famine that followed the failed agricultural reforms of the Great Leap Forward (1958–1961), one of Wu's father's uncle was among the nearly thirty million people who starved to death. His parents were therefore grateful that he had been given greater opportunities than they had experienced in their lives. Indeed, Wu Jiao was one of the lucky few; he had made it to a top university—though he was stuck in a life of routine and troubled by a sense of not having chosen his own direction. I do not mean to imply that Wu Jiao was leading his life fatalistically; rather, I was struck that a man in his twenties seemed to be placing his hopes in the next generation. As he put it, "Maybe our children will be happier; they should make their choices on their own." He gave the impression that his generation lacked a path it could call its own.

Next time we met, I asked Wu Jiao about his plans for changing his major and studying history instead, but he avoided my questions and turned the tables by asking me a lot of questions about how my research was progressing.

Perspectives

In this chapter, I have described from various perspectives the double binds of *suzhi jiaoyu*. The double bind of the Chinese state arises from its project of simultaneously wanting to create both citizens who are docile and loyal to their parents or nation and an elite of talented innovators who can make China more internationally competitive as a knowledge society. Just as Dewey's democratic ideals at the beginning of the twentieth century could not be easily reconciled with an authoritarian form of government, China's contemporary one-party-state places clear restrictions on the form and content of education. The project of *suzhi jiaoyu* to some extent seems to be a repetition of history—this time not as tragedy but as farce.[12]

Because of the limits that population size places on genuine opportunity, students and teachers alike see a contradiction between an ideology of self-actualization and a reality of restricted opportunity and limited freedom. In order to pass exams, get a degree, and succeed within the educational system, students have to withdraw from society and commit themselves to solitary study, immersing themselves in a world of books rather than involvement with other people (not unlike Mencius in the story recounted in my introduction). Only in this way can they hope to arrive at a point at which education provides them with the means to reciprocate the sacrifices their parents made to make higher education possible. However, success or self-realization is increasingly seen to require more than book learning within the walled and gated confines of a university campus.

Even though most students see *suzhi jiaoyu* as having little to do with social practice, the ideals of *suzhi jiaoyu* generally mirror the kind of "colorful" life that students long for as they struggle to escape the pressures of the educational system. Every individual finds himself or herself in competition with all of the other students who have made it to the top of the Chinese educational system, and this creates a rift between a desire to cultivate other qualities and a fear of falling behind. There is a contradiction between ideal and actual prospects, and many students fear it is possible to overcome this contradiction only by having recourse to nepotism and corruption. Some students regard test-based education as a more "democratic" way of ensuring that competition is fair. Others resort to fantasies about going abroad, escaping the pressure, and traveling from place to place like the American "boat guy."

Chapter 6
Success, Well-being, and the Question of Suicide

*You dare not injure your body, limbs, hair or skin, which you receive from your
father and mother.*

Confucius (551–479 BC), *Classic of Filial Piety*

ON A HOT JULY AFTERNOON IN 2007, I decided to take a taxi to Tsinghua University, where I had arranged to meet Liu Xing and visit the university's psychological counseling center. Liu Xing shared with me an interest in the gap between the university's policy of writing the cases of suicide off as "accidents" and the rumors and speculation that circulated among the students. While some students found it understandable that the universities should protect their reputations and avoid tabloid stories of elite students throwing themselves off tall buildings, others, like Liu Xing, felt the students had "a right to know what is going on."

On my way to the university, my taxi driver—a stout, chain-smoking middle-aged man—expressed curiosity about what I was doing in China and why I was going to Tsinghua University. I briefly told him about my research project and its focus on how Chinese university students cope with the pressures of education.

What pressure? University students are not under any pressure. High school students face a lot of pressure since they have to take the college entrance exams, and this will decide whether they will have a good future or not. The problem is that they [college students] are not responsible [*fuzeren*]. They go to the universities in order to find girlfriends and boyfriends instead of studying. But the idea of going to university is to study—not to find girlfriends and boyfriends, am I right?

I answered that I did not think it had to be a question of either/or. He then warned me against using Western concepts to understand China, a country with six thousand years of history! I decided to listen quietly, and he went on:

Let me give you another example of why young people are irresponsible. More and more young people do not want to have children after marriage, and some women even choose to live alone. It is their responsibility to have children—to continue the generational line. It is a problem that the excellent people [*you xiu ren*] are not producing children, whereas the backwards people, the peasants and the minorities, have many children. These "excellent people" have a duty to improve the Chinese population, so that in the future we will not only have six thousand years of history but eight thousand.

As he spoke, he indicated with a movement of his hand the ongoing progress of the Chinese people. When we arrived at the university, he gave me his phone number and urged me to call him if I needed any more help with my research.

Why are cases of suicide among elite university students so controversial? In this chapter I describe my attempts to address this sensitive issue.

A Public Secret

Liu Xing and I were politely received by a secretary at the psychological counseling center and seated on spacious mint-green couches in a cool, air-conditioned waiting room where we were served cups of green tea. After about an hour, one of the psychologists came to see us. After we had introduced ourselves, she told us that the center had been founded in 1988 as part of an effort to avoid student suicides.

The aim was to find and help students who were suffering from severe psychological problems, she explained. This was done by requiring all students to fill out questionnaires when enrolling at the university. These questionnaires served to reveal the psychological state of the students—their "psychological quality" (*xinli suzhi*). Furthermore, the center provided counseling for students with psychological problems and issued certificates enabling students to postpone an exam if they felt that they were under unbearable pressure. She said that two or three students a day received therapy, though more sought help during the exam periods.

When I asked her about cases of suicide among students, she said that she could not talk about specific cases; she could talk about the subject only in a general way. She saw the reasons for suicide as being connected to the pressures on singletons to live up to their parents' expectations.[1] She said that they were often referred to as "little emperors" or "little empresses" because they were materially spoiled but psychologically fragile and insecure. "It is hard for students who have been used to being top students in high school to have to compete suddenly with the best students from the whole country," she said. Furthermore, she said, problems in family relationships were often a contributing factor. She mentioned that research had been carried out on the high prevalence of rural women who commit suicide by poisoning themselves with pesticides, but added that although the center was gathering data on the subject, no "public" research had been done on suicide among students. She referred to the cases of suicide as a "public secret."

The notion of a "public secret" is in itself a contradiction in terms: how can something simultaneously be public and a secret? When I asked her to explain this, she said that the university did not want parents to worry, and that this was also government policy. Before Liu Xing and I arrived at the center, we had discussed how to approach the sensitive issue of suicide among students, and Liu Xing had urged me to ask direct questions. In her view this was the only way of obtaining any information.

Bearing Liu Xing's advice in mind, I asked the psychologist directly about the number of suicide cases at Tsinghua and whether this number was rising or falling. Her eyes flickered around the room before she replied, saying that there were very few suicides at Tsinghua. When I again insisted on asking how many cases there had been, she answered, "One or two over the past six or seven years." The real number is probably higher, since I had heard about more cases than that during the period of my fieldwork.

After we left the center and again found ourselves immersed in the suffocating humidity of the city, Liu Xing said, "I know for a fact that that is not true," reminding me that she had recently seen bloodstains on the pavement and cleaning people performing a ritual of purification.

The Fragility of Elite Students

I remember talking to one father in our neighborhood whose daughter had recently completed her college entrance examination and obtained a very high score. She could most probably enter Tsinghua University or Beijing University, he said, but he was pondering whether she should apply for a less high-ranking university, since he felt that there was a risk that "elite university students become crazy and kill themselves." His remark suggests a certain backlash to the fetishization of higher education in China. I would sometimes hear a comparison made between elite students and fragile glass—hard and refined on the outside but easily shattered by setbacks or failure. It is also worth noting that *suzhi jiaoyu* reforms are promoted on the grounds that they are necessary to reduce the pressure on young people that causes so many cases of suicide (Fong 2004:87; Kuan 2008:117). The intention is to try to remedy a situation in which the educational system is seen as producing fragile graduates of low "psychological quality" (*xinli suzhi*).

On one occasion, I had lunch with three professors who had offered to help with my research and had invited me for a meal of Japanese fast food at a busy off-campus restaurant. The atmosphere was relaxed, and after they had talked about their days as exchange students in Japan, how their children were doing, and who had and who hadn't been promoted, they asked me about my research. When I cautiously brought up the issue of suicide, the atmosphere became somewhat tense. Professor Wen said that he found all the talk about psychological pressure to be largely exaggerated. He emphasized that Chinese high school students like his own son faced a lot of pressure since the college entrance exams determined their future. However, students at Beijing and Tsinghua universities are the most fortunate students in China, he said. As far as he knew, most students were by and large happy and industrious, and felt lucky to have been given the chance to receive such an excellent education and enjoy the best facilities in China.[2]

After lunch, Professor Wen took us all for a ride around the Tsinghua campus in his black Audi, proudly showing me the modern architecture of the schools in the natural sciences. It was clear that he was trying to convey a model impression of a modern university—one that could be seen from a distance through the windows of a car driving through the campus.

Later that day, after Professor Wen had dropped us off at the metro station, the other members of our party and I stood in silence for a moment contemplating the setting sun, reddened by the polluted air. I was exhausted from trying to grasp and participate in many hours of conversation in Chinese. Xiao Hua, one of the female professors, broke the silence by talking about one of her students whom she was concerned about. She felt that her student was acting strangely and talking incoherently. I missed quite a lot of the ensuing conversation, but I was struck by the way they talked about the fragility of their students by saying they were porous, like eggs. I tried to enter into the conversation again, and Xiao Hua explained:

Young people are psychologically fragile. You could say that, like eggs, they can easily break, and there are many reasons for this. Because there are so many people in China, the pressure to do well is heavy. Parents urge their children to study, study, study to become excellent. In the past, maybe, learning three characters a day would be enough for little children. Today the situation is more complex. Parents also try to put more emphasis on the education of abilities such as learning musical instruments or drawing. Imagine that there are ten families living in the same building. Nine of them send their children to learn drawing, so what about the last family? They have no choice but to send their child to study drawing as well. And in this way, the pressure accelerates. Perhaps this situation is related to the process of development that China is in. After this period, perhaps people will become aware of these problems. Maybe there is going to be a time when there will be enough for everyone and people will not have to fight for their lives and the pressure will decrease.

The image of young people being fragile and porous like eggs brings to mind Mikkel Bunkenborg's description of the idea of porous persons, whose condition is likened to "a snowdrift on a mountainside that will turn into an avalanche at the slightest sound" (Bunkenborg 2009:199).[3] Bunkenborg describes the rapidly growing discourse about a condition known as sub-health (*yajiankang*) that has emerged over the last decade, reflecting concerns about the health or well-being of (in particular) the Chinese elite. The discourse holds that while people are not necessarily ill, they are not entirely healthy. This discourse has taken on a life of its own and has been adopted by pharmaceutical companies, which offer various remedies to improve individual health and competitiveness. Instances of sudden and inexplicable death are the most dramatic manifestations of the extreme stress experienced among the Chinese elite. Among the eager users of the new remedies are parents worried about their children's achievements (Bunkenborg 2009:199). This prevalent sense of a hidden but lethal flaw in the bodies of China's elite seems to be mirrored in the widespread anxieties about the psychological fragility of elite students that people expressed to me during my fieldwork.

Psychological Quality

Since students of elite universities make up the group of young people who have obtained the highest scores on the national college entrance exams, one would expect them to have the highest level of *suzhi*. According to Rachel Murphy, this is the case (Murphy 2004). However, the emphasis on the well-being of students, conceptualized through a focus on their "psychological quality," means that students from the top universities in some ways paradoxically epitomize the flaws of "test-based education."[4] As we shall see, the *suzhi jiaoyu* discourse is contradictory, since it is simultaneously focused on improving the quality and competitiveness of individuals and on reducing the pressure of competition.

The *suzhi jiaoyu* discourse, in other words, represents attempts both to reduce and to step up competition.

Returning for a moment to Xiao Hua's comment, let us consider how, when explaining the fragility of her students, she refers to their upbringing as only children who have been pressured by parents to do well and develop various talents. In *suzhi jiaoyu* parental guidance books, parents are urged to help their children develop other talents besides studying, but Xiao Hua sees this as creating excessive pressure on performing well in extracurricular interests. This makes *suzhi jiaoyu* problematic.

The relationship between social distinctions and well-being is complex. Gary Sigley has found that the *suzhi* discourse is attached to a hierarchy from "those who have the 'high quality' to govern themselves and those with 'low quality' who need to be governed by others and those somewhere in between." Although he does not mention the concept of "psychological quality," this expansion of the *suzhi* discourse seems to be an expression of his gloomy prediction that "under the conditions of the socialist market economy, the call found within technoscientific reasoning to create certain subjects does not diminish as one might expect; on the contrary, it intensifies and extends to many new realms of life" (Sigley 2009:558).

Suzhi therefore conveys the idea that the interiority of people can be improved, and that people can have higher or lower levels of psychological quality. The idea of psychological quality makes it almost impossible, however, to distinguish categorically between high and low, self-governing and in need of governance, since people of "high quality" may suffer from a lack of "psychological quality," and this can ultimately lead to suicide. Such individuals are therefore in need of therapy to help them govern themselves better. Here, one must discount the question of whether this is a form of neoliberalism or not, since a categorical term like *suzhi* does not allow one to reduce the personal to the cultural or to assume that people participating in the same economy or educational system never call their lives into question.

The Dream of Harvard

Gu Wei was a third-year Tsinghua student in computer engineering who hailed from Changsha in Hunan province. He looked younger than his twenty-three years and had a tick in one of his eyes. Both his parents were civil servants, whom he described as "not very successful in their careers." His father was among the first students allowed to take the college entrance exams after the end of the Cultural Revolution, and he had a degree in engineering. His mother had attended a technical secondary school. When I met Gu Wei he was taking leave from his studies, since he had been unable to cope with the pressure. As we sat opposite each other sipping jasmine tea among hundreds of empty orange plastic chairs in one of Tsinghua University's huge dining halls during a break between eating hours, our conversation revolved around his mother. "My mother used to plan my life a lot," Gu Wei said.

She is a typical Chinese mother. She chose my middle school, my high school, and she wanted me to enter Tsinghua University. As a child I didn't like the way she was so strict with me, always telling me to study and not to play, but I more or less followed her demands. Even though I did not find it interesting, I just followed the way and I did well in the college entrance examination and I entered Tsinghua University.

Gu Wei explained that like many students at Tsinghua, he was not really interested in his major. His mother was happy that he had entered Tsinghua University, but planned for him to obtain a master's degree in the United States so that he could return to China and find a good job. He attempted to pursue this path, but after several failed attempts he began suffering from chronic headaches and insomnia. He described how he would lie awake, tossing and turning in the bunk of his dorm, seeing English phrases flying around the room. He had contacted the psychological counseling center of the university and had been able to postpone some of his exams.

When I asked how his mother had reacted, Gu Wei said, "This came as a big surprise to me. She said that she was sure that I had done my best and that no one would blame me for postponing my exams. I hadn't expected her to be so understanding." Reflecting on why his mother had been so uncompromising and harsh in urging him to study, he continued, "I think she felt that she had no choice. There are so many people in China, and if you don't do well you will have no future. The government . . . I mean the parents . . . feel that there is no other way." He added that his mother had not had the opportunity to go to university herself and that she was not very happy about her own life and did not like her work. She was not good at handling social relationships within the party, he said. Therefore she wanted him to have a better life, and she saw education as the only way of achieving this. When I asked him about his father, he responded that most of the time he was busy earning money for the family.

It seems that for most of his life—or at least this is how he saw it in retro-spect—Gu Wei had been following "the way." However, he had been through a crisis, and the stress had manifested in physical symptoms. The work by Arthur and Joan Kleinman on somatization may shed light on Gu Wei's headaches and dizziness. According to the Kleinmans, dizziness and headaches, or *tou yun*, resonate with a central metaphor in Chinese medicine, namely balance or har-mony between macrocosm and microcosm, and between the constituents of the body/self and the social world (Kleinman and Kleinman 1996:177–178). Even though the situation of the so-called "lost generation," who suffered from the vi-olence and injustices of the Cultural Revolution, cannot be compared with the situation of students like Gu Wei, who have grown up with greater opportuni-ties for education, both involve a loss of balance between personal aspirations and the expectations of others. Whereas the sufferers of the Cultural Revolution experienced dizziness, exhaustion, and sleeplessness as a result of months of working frenetically in political campaigns, it could be argued that Gu Wei's psychosomatic symptoms express his own disenchantment with what he calls "following the way"—trying to satisfy his parents' (mother's) aspirations for him, but finding himself caught up in a process of studying for exams to the point where he could no longer sleep and saw English phrases flying around in the room whenever he closed his eyes.

However, this crisis led to greater rapport between Gu Wei and his mother. When he failed to live up to her expectation that he go abroad for further study, he felt that he understood his mother better. "My mother used to plan my life a lot," he said, using the past tense, as if this was no longer the case. Oddly enough, his inability to live up to his mother's expectations alleviated the pres-sure he had been under.

One day while Gu Wei and I were having lunch together, he smiled at me and said, "Actually, talking to you is for me a form of *suzhi jiaoyu*." His remark took me by surprise. He explained that through his talks with a psychologist at the counseling center at his university, he had been advised to do other things besides just study for the sake of his personal development (*fazhan ziji*). He ex-plained that he thought talking to a foreigner, such as me, might be a way of im-proving his "social skills." During the fall of 2007 we met regularly, and I followed his quest for self-development. While we were walking across the campus one day it started to rain heavily, and as we made our way through a crowd of um-brellas that quickly appeared, seemingly out of nowhere, we discussed whether this was natural rain or rain that had been artificially induced by shooting the clouds with chemicals, which sometimes happened. Gu Wei suggested that we should have lunch at a Western café off campus, since he wanted to challenge himself by trying something new.

I can clearly picture him, sitting in front of me, self-consciously struggling to eat with a knife and fork instead of the familiar chopsticks, and reflecting on how difficult it was for him to pursue his own interests, since he did not know what they might be. "I wish I had some special talent, or something I knew I would really like to do. I admire people who have this quality, but I am really not sure what I am interested in," he said. When he was a child, his mother had urged him to take piano lessons. "But the other students were so diligent," he said, "so I soon lost interest." He explained that the psychologist had suggested that he take some other courses as a way of developing his "psychological quality" as well as his "quality of life," advising him that "life is more than just studying." He asked me how I would define "quality of life." I was surprised by this question and said that I did not know how to define it. Instead, I asked him whether or not there was something or other that might improve his mood. He answered, "Night talk," a reference to the conversations that sometimes took place among the youths in his dormitory after lights-out. Although he had previously told me that he was reluctant to talk to his peers about his problems, and although he had described his relationship to them as highly ambiguous, since he could not understand how they could do well when they spent so much of their time playing computer games, he said that "talking about all kinds of things" improved his mood.

In fact Gu Wei attended several *suzhi jiaoyu* courses, including a course on "developing one's psychological potential." I took part in some of these classes with him. In this series of lectures, issues of suicide and coping with the pressures of competition were brought up. The course provided the students with management strategies for how best to plan one's time. It also urged students to focus on relaxing activities, such as sports, music, and art. The students appeared to lack any enthusiasm for this course, and several in fact slept on their chairs. During recess, other students told me that this was an easy course, but a bit of a waste of time, since their time could be better spent working on courses that needed more effort to pass. The course was taught by one of the psychologists from the psychological counseling center of the university, and she had let me participate in it. But when I expressed an interest in visiting the center, she apologized for being busy and said she would get back to me.

Gu Wei also had attended a course titled "The Appreciation of Famous Universities at Home and Abroad." He described this as a course in which students watched films about famous foreign universities, and he recalled with some fascination having watched a film about Harvard. Though captivated by the beautiful campus, where groups of young people sat together on a lush green lawn under a clear blue sky, so different from Beijing's polluted air, he still found the course to be a waste of time. "I would have liked to go to Harvard to study," he said, "but what could I possibly learn from watching a film about Harvard? It only made me more depressed." He had also attempted to take piano classes, but ironically he found this to be yet another competitive field. "Several hundred people applied for the class, and only twenty could attend," he said. "But at least I tried," Gu Wei added with a shrug of his shoulders.

Gu Wei's experience clearly shows that one of the paradoxes of the *suzhi jiaoyu* discourse is that it attempts to displace a structural problem onto individual personality. Is the problem one of an inner deficiency of the individual, or is it a result of scarce possibilities produced by the *outer* structures of a competitive educational system?

Paradoxically, attempts to reform the Chinese educational system in accordance with the ideas of *suzhi jiaoyu* all too easily end up reinforcing what the policy is meant to change. As Xiao Hua put it, "The pressure accelerates." In a sense, the dream (or nightmare) of aspiring to a scholarship to Harvard is both the source of and the proposed cure for his problems. He had been unable to reach his (mother's) goal of going abroad for further study, and had suffered from psychosomatic symptoms as a result of excessive pressure. In his attempt to manage and alleviate his anxieties, he had taken a course on how to cope with pressure. This course promoted *suzhi jiaoyu*–based ideas, including the recommendation that he experience other things in life besides study. It soon became apparent to him that foreign travel, to Harvard in particular, was the ultimate expression of *suzhi jioayu*. In other words, he faced a catch-22, and it seemed to him that in the global race for competitiveness in a knowledge economy, the means precluded any critical evaluation of the ends.

Gu Wei felt that there was no way of escaping the pressure and said that he could understand those who committed suicide:

In high school we used to ask ourselves, why we should go to school when school means suffering. But suffering is necessary in order to get a better life. The more you suffer, the more you will gain. Now I have realized that this is not necessarily true. Some of the best students are the ones who work the least, and after graduation I know that I may make a lot of money, but I will still have no time to do the things I like. An accountant works twenty hours a day. Only death is the end of suffering.

The Precariousness of Experience

Is my account of the *suzhi jiaoyu* reforms too biased and bleak? It is possible that I have been drawn more to the problems and contradictions that people struggle with than to stories of success. So it is appropriate to mention here that some students do appreciate *suzhi jiaoyu* courses and manage to find a balance between work and play, duty and leisure, and are relatively satisfied with their situation. Helen, for instance, sang in the university choir, and even though this entailed taking part in a competition between universities, she said that the most important thing was that they really enjoyed singing together. "Even though we don't all have exceptionally beautiful voices, together we can really accomplish something great." She added, "Singing in the choir relieves me of the pressure."

Let me return to the work of the existential psychologist R. D. Laing, particularly his reference to the famous gestalt image of the vase-cum-face. Although there is only one image on the paper, we will identify two different objects (a vase or two faces) depending on how the image appears to us at any given moment. By invoking this equivocal or ambiguous figure, Laing wants to point out that we see others in quite different ways—as multidimensional persons or as biological organisms—depending on our pre-understandings and our interests (Laing [1960] 1983:20–21). Potentially, a medical professional may view a schizophrenic in a depersonalized way through what Laing calls "it-processes," or as another human being.

Following Laing's reasoning, I suggest that there is a difference between expressing concern for a person's *well-being* and seeking to improve a person's *psychological quality*. Existentially, this corresponds to the difference between treating the other as an object (characterized by some inner lack) and treating the other as a person (who is irreducible to his or her particular incapacity).

Merleau Ponty used a gestalt model to point out that consciousness constantly shifts between figure and ground. What is visible carries with it a sense of other things that are co-present but backgrounded and shadowy (Jackson 1995:160). This perspective is reminiscent of Hannah Arendt's comments on the slippage between being a *who* and a *what* (Arendt 1958:8). The psychologist of the university's counseling center urged Gu Wei to engage in activities that would improve his psychological quality. Even though Gu Wei made the ironic comment that meeting with me, a foreigner, was a form of *suzhi jiaoyu*, a way of helping him develop his "social skills," in practice this was probably not the entire reason. It seems likely that there is an oscillation between means and ends—that is, a slippage between being a *who* and being a *what*. At different times people may see the goals differently. *Suzhi jioayu* has perhaps the potential to be both, and at different times one perspective may be either figure or ground.

Phrased differently, intersubjectivity reflects the way our awareness continuously drifts between transitive and intransitive extremes, so that a person is sometimes fulfilled by being with another and at other times engulfed by the will of another (James 1950:296–297).

This cybernetic shifting of perspectives clearly came across in Gu Wei's changing views on his situation. At times he experienced the imperative for self-realization as disempowering. It made him feel insecure since he did not know "what he was really interested in," or how he could "improve his psychological quality." At other times, what he seemed to foreground more was his struggle to act on his situation.[5] He was trying out alternatives, and although he was skeptical of these attempts, he was at least doing something about finding his own path in life. Drawing on the work of Viktor Frankl, Jackson argues that an existential precondition for well-being is a sense of hope, a feeling that there is a way out, and that this is related to the experience of being able to act upon a situation (Jackson, unpublished manuscript[6]).

At times Gu Wei seemed to have no hope for the future, declaring that only suicide could end the pressure. At other times he was more hopeful, as when he told me about the relief he experienced when he realized that his mother did in fact love him unconditionally, regardless of whether or not he obtained a scholarship to an American university. However, the question of whether self-development or self-realization was the source of his problems or a solution to his problems remains open.

Furthermore, as Viktor Frankl has argued, since a pre-condition for well-being is a sense of being-with-others, by implication well-being, self-realization, or quality of life cannot be found within oneself, but only in relation to significant others (Jackson 2011:364–367). This can be read in Gu Wei's story, as well as in some of the other stories of this chapter and Chapter 5, where well-being was described as "night talk," singing in a choir, or falling in love.

Suicide as Social Critique

Let me return to the act of suicide that I broached in my introduction.

In April 2005 a twenty-year-old student at Beijing University wrote this message on the university intranet before she leaped to her death:

I made a List

Put reasons to live on the left side

Reasons to die on the right

I wrote many things on the right

But found little to write on the left

Not willing to imagine

Continuing to live like this for decades.

I mentioned earlier that while the official stance of the university was to pass this incident off as an accident, it crept into conversations among students and on the intranet. While some students regarded suicide as absurd and tragic given that students of elite universities are so fortunate in comparison with many other Chinese university students, others readily understood what this twenty-one-year-old meant about her "unwillingness to go on living like this." While many students speculated about why an individual should choose death over life, none seemed to question the rational phrasing of the note. In my view, what is so uncanny about these last lines is that they indicate that the suicide was not at all spontaneous, but rather carefully planned and rationally thought through, by calculating whether the reasons to live outweighed the reasons to die. Tragically, few reasons could be listed on the left. It is impossible to know what this person had in mind when writing this note, but it seems to mirror the notion that quality of life can be objectively assessed.

Let me approach the issue by considering the social and cultural discourses about suicide in China, where there is a long-standing tradition of suicide as social protest (Wu 2005). In the view of Professor Wen, as well as that of the talkative taxi driver, elite university students were not subjected to significant pressure, let alone driven to commit suicide. However, both mentioned the well-known phenomenon of the pressure on Chinese high school students when they take the college entrance exams.

An example of such a case was published in the *New York Times* of August 1, 2004. The article concerns a young Chinese man, Qingming, who, having just learned that he could not take part in the college entrance exams, threw himself under an approaching train in his rural village (cited in Biehl, Good, and Kleinman 2007:2). Lacking the money required to take the exam, Qingming fled this school and wandered around the village. Later, some villagers commented that he had talked about working for Interpol. The authorities later used this to support the view that Qingming was mentally ill, though his grandfather subsequently filed a lawsuit against the school, insisting that the healthy young man he had raised was "upset, not mentally ill." The grandfather found a scrapbook made by his grandson, in which Qingming had pasted a magazine article about a young girl who had been raped and abandoned by her relatives because of the shame she had brought upon them. In the margin, Qingming had written: "We must extend our helping hand to any innocent underdog. Only by so doing can that person find a footing in society" (cited in Biehl, Good, and Kleinman 2007:2).

The case of Qingming's suicide supports the view that suicide is a form of social protest, an extreme reaction to oppressive circumstances. Wu Fei has conducted a comprehensive study of suicide in rural China in which he argues that it is mainly a response to domestic injustice. In particular, he found suicide among rural women to be a reaction to oppressive family relationships, and he writes against what he sees as a Western tradition[7] of seeing suicide as primarily resulting from a malaise of the social body[8] (Durkheim 1952) or from depression or other psychiatric or psychological problems.[9] Instead, he emphasizes the long tradition in China of viewing suicide in relation to power struggles and social injustice. In traditional China, suicides among daughters-in-law were frequent and may be interpreted as ways of gaining "face" after death, or being recognized as a full person in relation to a powerful and oppressive mother-in-law in a patrilineal kinship structure.[10] According to Wu, "Psychologically most people consider themselves as full persons, but sociologically beggars, the disabled, the mentally ill and retarded as well as prostitutes are considered nonpersons" (Wu 2005:218). By implication, personhood is never stable but has to be struggled for or consolidated through power games in which one person is pitted against another. In these games, face and personhood can be lost.

In a similar vein, Wu argues that when people commit suicide in contemporary China, it is a response to a felt injustice when the balance of power within the conjugal family tips against them. Suicide is a revolt against a situation in which one is not regarded as "a full person." Wu explores how suicide is understood not only in the domestic sphere but also in the public sphere, where, he argues, suicide reflects dilemmas intrinsic to the Chinese modernity project. Despite the disappearance of the patrilineal family structure and the prevalence of conjugal ties, ideas about personhood, shame, and stigma persist, creating "non-persons" who cannot change their social status (Wu 2005:345).[11]

Given this tradition of viewing suicide as a response to social injustice, how can it be that young elite students, who are in a position that others envy, sometimes decide to take their own lives? A conclusive answer to this question lies outside the scope of this book, but I think it becomes clear why these cases of suicide constitute a taboo.[12] The aim of the one-child policy was to create a highly educated population that would modernize China. As I have shown throughout the book, the educational system is deeply affected by cultural notions of sacrifice, both in relations between the generations and in those between young people and the state. Parents make great sacrifices by investing care, energy, and resources in their child, in the hope that he or she will receive a good education and will in turn work diligently in order to do well, thereby reciprocating the parental sacrifices and fulfilling the generational contract. The Chinese state also invests considerable resources in the education of elite university students. As was often pointed out to me, the two universities I studied have a disproportionate amount of the national educational budget at their disposal. However, as I have argued throughout the book, returns on these investments are by no means guaranteed, and people face uncertainty about when and if their investments will pay off, or if their sacrifices were worth making.

I think it reasonable to suggest that student suicides are deeply troubling to people because they call into question the logic of sacrifice as a modality of intersubjectivity, and of the intergeneration continuity of *yang*. As Charles Stafford observes, "Even a patriotic suicide or any other premature death is problematic for a kinship ideology based on unbroken descent and long life as 'the flow of yang' is made discontinuous" (Stafford 1995:114). For parents, a child's suicide is the worst that could befall them. Thus, when Jing Jing attempted to commit suicide, her mother bowed down to perform a traditional kowtow (*ketou*), begging her never again to attempt to take her own life. In this act, the customary relationship between parent and child was inverted, and Jing Jing became aware of the devastating effect that her suicide would have had on her mother's life. Other students, such as Gu Wei, told me that the thought of taking their own lives had sometimes occurred to them, but that this was something they could never do to their parents. For the state, cases of suicide by elite students entail the annihilation of a superior birth, thus challenging the quasi-religious belief in the power of elite education as the way toward prosperity and social harmony for the Chinese family and the nation.

Another double-bind may be discerned here. On the one hand, self-sacrifice and self-interest are intimately connected, since sacrifices are carried out in accordance with a promise of future return. On the other hand, as a form of self-effacement, sacrifice logically entails the extreme possibility of self-annihilation, or suicide (Jackson 1998:73). A moral dilemma, or *aporia*, is hereby created: while young people are expected to make sacrifices, they are not expected to sacrifice themselves to such an extent as to negate their very existence. The psychologist I interviewed at Tsinghua saw a clear connection between the idea of the only child as a "little emperor" and the troubled psychology of elite students.

To what extent is the Chinese state, and the covenant between parents and state in China, responsible for the so-called "little emperor" syndrome? This question is suggested by the fact that historically, "China's little emperors" were spoiled both in the imperial courts and within the family. Even today, Chinese children are under tremendous pressure to "serve their parents," as well as to "serve the state or society" by living up to high expectations, developing into "people of quality," and thereby increasing the power, status, and welfare of the nation. The term "emperor" is in itself ambiguous because it is invoked by the Communist Party to repudiate the imperial past, yet perpetuates this imperial order through the hegemony of the one-party Communist state.

According to Charles Stafford, "Putting oneself at risk for the nation is actually seen as the highest form of Confucian ethics" (Stafford 1995:114). One such example is found in the story "Virtuous Mothers of Ancient Times": "Yue Fei was a famous hero of the people [*minzu de yingxiong*] who grew up in extreme poverty. His mother used branches and wrote in the sand in order to teach him, and also encouraged him to carefully develop his strength, hoping that in future he would become a master of the pen and the sword [*wenwu shuanquan de rencai*]."

Although Yue Fei's scholarly and military talents were exceptional, his mother further encouraged him to dedicate himself (*baoxiao*) to the nation, etching the characters "repay the nation with utter loyalty" (*jinzhong baogao*) on his back. Yue Fei dared not to forget his mother's instructions, and later had many great victories in battle, recovering lost territories, redressing the nation's humiliation, and earning the greatest admiration of the people (*renmen de zongjing*) (cited in Stafford 1995:114).

Stafford points out that that the term *baogao* means "repay the nation" or "dedicate oneself to the nation," and contains the same *bao* that appears in the word used to describe the "paying back" (*baoda*) of parents for their sacrifices and care (Stafford 1995:114). In the case of martyrdom, sacrifice is meaningful, for though a person dies, the ideal that he or she espoused is given greater life (Jackson 2009:205). But elite students who commit suicide are not martyrs because their deaths enable no ideal to be confirmed or celebrated. Because a person's individual *shen* (body person) embodies the happiness of the family and the greatness of the nation, the suicide of high-quality children renders the notion of sacrifice meaningless. In fact, such a suicide implies a critique of the social order.

The question of whether the elite students who committed suicide intended a social critique cannot be conclusively answered, but the fact that many student suicides involve jumping off a high university building may suggest that suicide is a public statement—a rejection of the gift of life and a repudiation of education as the means of self-fulfillment. Parents expect their children to outgrow and eventually replace them, but if a child refuses to grow up or, worse, takes his or her own life, this natural course of time is broken. Before she jumped to her death, the girl who wrote a suicide note on the Beijing University intranet clearly rejected the future, saying that she was "unwilling to go on living like this for decades."

Sherry Ortner's reflections on the relativity of the term "success" are relevant here, since she points out that success is interpreted differently according to a person's biography: "Success is always comparative. One is always more or less successful in relation to others. But even more importantly, one is more or less successful compared with where one started—one's family background, one's experiences growing up, opportunities seized or not" (Ortner 2003:5).

Similarly, Amartya Sen has pointed out that inequality is not entirely reducible to socioeconomic factors, but involves existential issues and differs from person to person: "You could be well-off, without being well. You could be well, without being able to lead the life you wanted. You could have got the life you wanted, without being happy. You could be happy, without having much freedom. You could have a good deal of freedom without achieving much" (Sen 1988:1).

Although the students of China's top universities often seemed dispirited and under great pressure, their sense of success and well-being was highly variable—from person to person, from moment to moment, and from one stage of their life to another. Sometimes, sacrifices did not seem worthwhile and the hoped-for rewards were not forthcoming. Sometimes, students recalled the sacrifices they had made, the pressures they had subjected themselves to, and the disciplines imposed on them by parents and the educational system, and saw it all as worthwhile, since they had achieved outstanding results. The end had justified the means. But others experienced only disappointment, dashed dreams, and dissatisfaction.

Conclusion

IN THIS BOOK I have described what it is like to grow up in a society in which dramatic economic progress has gone hand in hand with a concerted effort to create a talented elite that will make the nation prosper and rise to power. Students at Tsinghua and Beijing universities clearly experienced the weight of great expectations, and for many the fetishization of education came at a cost. This educational pressure is not likely to diminish in the near future. Rather, it may increase. People often express the concern that since there are so many people in China, there is unfortunately no way of escaping the pressure, which continues to accelerate and take on new and more complex forms. The efforts to alleviate pressure through *suzhi jiaoyu* are most often dismissed as a pipe dream. And even though the college entrance exams are dreaded by the entire society, since they are imagined to mark the difference between a life worth living and a life not worth living, it is also the case that they are perceived as a necessary evil. Any alternative ways of selecting who gets the chance to become part of the talented elite seem arbitrary and less democratic.

Zachary Howlett cites a high school principal from southeastern China who said, "If we didn't have *gao kao* there would be social revolution in China" (Howlett, forthcoming). In other words, the college entrance examinations can be seen as an "instituted fantasy" (Sangren 2013). Although ultimately unrealizable for most people, the exams create the illusion that everyone has a fair chance at beating the odds. The paradox is thus that even the students who have excelled on the exam and have entered China's top universities, thus epitomizing the Chinese dream of social mobility through higher education, often suffered from excessive pressure, from melancholia, or from a sense of not having had a say in choosing their own life path. I have argued that success and well-being are not synonymous, since an existential precondition for well-being is a sense of hope, a feeling that there is a way out, and that this is related to the experience of being able to act upon a situation.

Some students have been cramming and working hard for years, trying to live up to external expectations, only to find that they are running to nowhere. A telling comment came from a student watching a high-rise train from above, who noted that everybody seems to rush ahead in order to get on the train and not be left behind, but no one seems to reflect on where the train is going. The comment brings home the way in which means sometimes become so important that the ends are forgotten.

By focusing on sacrifice as a critical theme, I have brought into relief some of the tensions, contradictions, and double binds that my young interlocutors face. On the one hand, students accept a degree of self-denial, cramming for exams and coping with competition, but on the other hand they want to feel personally fulfilled in their everyday lives. In some cases, they experienced hard work and diligence as necessary, even fulfilling, sacrifices, but very often their efforts to become successful led to insecurity, dissatisfaction, and in some instances, despair. However, sacrifice is a mode of reciprocity, which means that sacrifice and self-interest are not always mutually incompatible. Gaining requires giving, and self-realization entails self-sacrifice. Moreover, self-realization can, paradoxically, be found only in relationship to others. This means that the calculation of what must be given in order to gain self-realization or success is never straightforward, but must be negotiated throughout the course of intersubjective life.

Young people such as Zhou Lemin and Wu Liang, who recalled their childhoods as characterized by self-sacrifices—solitary studying, severe discipline, a lack of playtime—eventually came to terms with their parents' strict upbringing, concluding that "there was no other way." Today they express gratitude to the parents who forced them to study diligently, seeing that now as enabling them to enter a top university and to envision a better life than their parents had.

Students from China's rural areas have grown up under less pressure from their parents. Having made it into an elite university in the capital of the country, they have undergone a "class journey," and in the process have acquired a greater sense of self-determination. Yet this has come at a price, since they feel estranged from their parents' lifeworlds, though compelled to take care of them during their old age. And so they ask themselves how they can fulfill their filial obligations without compromising their own ambitions, since to remain in their hometown may doom them to the same poverty in which their parents have lived, and caring for them in their old age may mean the abandonment of their own dreams. Young people such as Sun Li and Bai Gang express great affection for their parents; they feel obliged to respect them and do not want to hurt their feelings. Yet they cannot wholly escape a sense of looking down on them, identifying them as primitive peasants or villagers who have little knowledge of the world and only a limited view of what life has to offer. Can higher education and future remittances compensate for the rupture of familial bonds? There is no clear answer to this question. This unresolvable oedipal dilemma of how much one owes one's parents (or the past) and how much one owes oneself (and the future) often centers on education, and informs the project of modernity everywhere.

The double bind of the Chinese state springs from its paying lip service to Western-style innovation while remaining an authoritarian state anxious to keep control. The state thus encourages both innovation and conformity. It wishes to create filial young citizens who are loyal to both their parents and the nation. At the same time, there is a realization that diligent and docile citizens do not necessarily have what it takes in order to succeed in a brave new knowledge society.

President Xi Jinping's vague slogan "The Chinese Dream" attempts to overcome this double bind by addressing the future through invoking China's glorious past before the "hundred years of humiliation."[1] In his acceptance speech at the National People's Congress, Xi Jinping stated that young people should "dare to dream, work assiduously to fulfill the dreams and contribute to the revitalization of the nation." The following day the party's propaganda chief ordered that the concept be written into school textbooks to make sure that it "entered students' brains." According to the party's theoretical journal *Qiushi*, the Chinese Dream, which seems to mimic the American Dream, is about Chinese prosperity, collective effort, socialism, and national glory. But nonetheless, the way to achieve this seems to be through individual striving. To what extent can personal desires and nationalist demands be reconciled, so that self-development is consistent with becoming a good citizen?

Most students, also those who were party members, dismissed the language of the party as empty rhetoric. Students such as Ryan, Liu Xing, and Wu Jiao imagined America as a space of freedom from parental, state, and government control, a place in which self-realization could be achieved. Helen, who had been to London as an intern, returned to Beijing with a British boyfriend and critical views of the Chinese political system and its lack of democratic rights. Liu Xing also imagined America as an avenue for self-realization, yet did not want her own future children to forget their national roots, mother tongue, and family commitment. She was caught between Chinese and American utopias. Eventually, she returned to China to be a filial daughter, though estranged from the homeland she had left.

The fantasy of America or of the affluent and liberal West is reminiscent of Bourdieu's notion of *illusio*, which encompasses all those "well-founded illusions" in which people place their hopes, or discover a sense of purpose or a promise of well-being (Bourdieu 1990). But as Ernst Bloch has pointed out in his work on hope, utopia (*ou-topos*) is literally "no-where" (Bloch 1986:1–17). It can perhaps be captured in the little word "yonder," which, according to Siri Hustvedt, is "neither here nor there" (Hustvedt 1998:1). The Chinese project of seeking to create citizens of high quality by emulating the West is clearly not a one-way street. Ann Hulbert has pointed out that "even as American educators seek to emulate Asian pedagogy—a test-centered ethos and a rigorous focus on math, science and engineering—Chinese educators are trying to blend a Western emphasis on critical thinking, versatility and leadership into their own traditions" (Hulbert 2007:5).

Put differently, the problems inherent in Chinese higher education clearly have wider implications. As Aihwa Ong has argued, institutions such as MIT, with a central science focus, are models for the university of the future (Ong 2006:155–156). She suggests that there is a crisis of the humanities not only in American universities but also globally. In the face of global competitiveness, one sometimes fears that the balance between a humanistic conception of higher education as an end in itself and the technicist conception of education as a means to an end may be lost, and any public critical conversation about these "ends" may come to be regarded as irrelevant or retrograde.

By focusing on double binds or *aporias*, I have tried to highlight the kinds of existential dilemmas my interlocutors sometimes faced, and the situations in which it was simply not possible to have it both ways. These dilemmas provide a window to understanding the rapidly changing Chinese society, but they also point to an aspect of the human condition in the sense that we all struggle to reconcile competing demands between ourselves and those we care about, as well as between what we want and what is decided by wider social and political forces over which we often have little or no control. And yet people's experiences are never reducible to the policies or external demands that affect them. The Taoist image[2] of a human being in a boat between two towering cliffs brings forth both the fragility and the resilience of human lives as lying in the capacity and urge to have some say over one's own life even if this takes the form of making adjustments from moment to moment between the ideal and the possible.

Notes

Introduction

1. The fieldwork for this book was carried out in 2005 and 2007 as well as during a brief period in the summer of 2012. Through the help of an anonymous student, I put up a poster at the intranet of both Tsinghua University and Beijing University (Beida) asking students to take part in my research project on the lives of Chinese students and I received an overwhelming number of e-mails from students who were willing to meet with me and share their life stories and personal experiences. I also took part in some classes and spent time with them inside and outside of the campuses.

2. Official Chinese statistics on this matter are not available, but according to Paul Mooney, she was one of seventeen college students in Beijing who committed suicide during the first seven months of that year (Mooney 2005:1).

3. The sociologist Karl Mannheim was the first to address the problem of categorizing generations in his famous essay "The Problem of Generations" ([1927] 1952). Since people are constantly being born and dying, when does one generation end and a new one begin? He systematized the idea of historical generations, or the generation as a cohort, thus shifting the focus from biological age to the "location" of age within history: people born in the same period of time share common experiences, potentials, and "destinies." Within cohorts, "generation units" represent subcategories who "work up the material of their common experiences in different specific ways." The study of historical change therefore shows how change occurs unevenly, since "differences and conflicts are found both within generations and between them" (Mannheim [1927] 1952:304).

4. For Aristotle the movement to the public sphere (*polis*) also went through the family sphere (*domus*). Politik ([1946] 1997:76–77)1.2.125124-b39.

5. It discussed the different stages of childhood, and what adults can expect of children and begin to teach them. In the first year, a baby should be taught to use his or her right hand, in the third year a child should be taught how to reply appropriately to adults, in the sixth year a child should be taught numerals and the names of the points on the compass, and so on (Bai 2005:16, cited in Kuan 2008).

6. As Greenhalgh has pointed out, the Communist Party needed to redefine birth control as a Marxist activity. It therefore adapted several strategies in this regard, including noting the importance of "planning" to socialism, and labeling the desire for many or male

children as feudal and an activity disavowing Malthus, whom Marx had criticized as being "capitalist" (Greenhalgh 2003). Under Chinese socialism, the idea is that having too many people does not necessarily lead to Malthusian misery, as the productive forces of society develop and are fairly distributed. Rather, the issue is redefined as the relationship between population quantity and population quality. In order to improve the quality of the population, its quantity must be controlled first. In this way the rationale of the one-child policy is that having an abundance of children makes it impossible to devote unlimited attention to each of them.

7. The term is difficult to translate into English, since although in English one may speak of human "qualities," it is dehumanizing to use the singular form to discuss "the quality" of an individual. Though one may speak of the moral qualities of a person using the term "character," the mental qualities using the term "intelligence," and the psychical qualities using the term "strength," there is no term like *suzhi* that can refer to all of these things at once (Kipnis 2006:304). As the modern nature/nurture dichotomy influenced Chinese thought during the twentieth century, the term became associated with inborn characteristics and it could then be contrasted with the word *suyang*, which refers to embodied characteristics that result from a person's upbringing (Kipnis 2006:297). Since the 1970s, the term has undergone a transformation. *Suzhi* no longer connotes the natural in a nature/nurture dichotomy, but connotes individually embodied human qualities. The concept of *suzhi* is slippery and not easily definable, but it bears a resemblance to the German *Bildung*, which entails aspects of distinction and class.

8. The Chinese word for education (*jiaoyu*) can be divided into three components: family education (*jiating jiaoyu*), school education (*xue xiao jiaoyu*), and the broader category of social education (*shehui jiaoyu*), which refers to the wider social context in which education takes place (Woronov 2007:30).

9. For more on ancestral sacrifice and state ritual practices in late imperial China, see Zito (1994).

10. The character *xiao* 孝 is composed of two other characters: the top half of the character *lao* 老 ("old") and the character *zi* 子 ("son"). When the two are combined to constitute *xiao*, the "old" is on top of the "son," or the elder on top of the younger. The ideograph can be taken to mean that the old are supported by the young. It can also be taken to mean that the young are oppressed by the old. Since Chinese used to be written from top to bottom, it can also simply be taken to imply that filial piety is the continuation of the family line (Ikels 2004:3).

11. This relationship is played out differently in different societies. In Europe there is a flow of resources from old to young within the family, and from young to old in state pension schemes. Only a few African states provide pensions for all senior citizens; most often older people are taken care of by their children when they are unable to take care of themselves (Alber, van der Geest, and Whyte 2008).

12. According to Michael Jackson, a long-standing cliché about existential anthropology is that it is preoccupied with the fate of individuals cast into a world they had no hand in choosing. They are not assured of any God-given or natural meanings for existence, and

yet are obliged to assume responsibility for themselves and their fellow human beings and wrest some sense out of the absurd situation in which they find themselves. "Defined in this way existentialism seems to offer nothing for anthropologists whose work takes us into lifeworlds where individuality is often played down, where a person's fate is often decided by forces outside his comprehension and control, where identity is defined less in being than in belonging, where ultimate meaning is associated with God, spirits and ancestors, where death is never final, and where one's main responsibility is not to oneself but to others" (Jackson 2005:xi–xii).

13. Here I am paraphrasing Charles Stafford's "The Roads of Chinese Childhood," in which the metaphor of two roads refers to both *remaining* something, through protecting what is seen to be a natural process of securing kinship and national identification, and *becoming* something, through a more "Confucian" emphasis on learning and self-cultivation (Stafford 1995:17–18). The two roads thus point to learning as what takes place *outside* school as well as *in* school. My context is in many ways different (focused on university rather than primary-school level, and placed in mainland China rather than in Taiwan), so I am merely borrowing the metaphor in order to point to the existential tension between different social imperatives that have to do with processes of separation and attachment.

14. "Each culture contains the negation of its manifest pattern and nuclear values, through a tacit affirmation of contrary latent patterns and marginal values. The complete real pattern of a culture is a product of a functional interplay between officially affirmed and officially negated patterns possessing mass" (Devereux 1967:212).

15. As Plato used the term, it referred to a logical conundrum that left Plato's interlocutors numb or speechless. This is perhaps most famously depicted in Socrates' conversation with Menon, where Socrates three times leaves him speechless, since he contradicts his attempts to arrive at a clear definition of "goodness" (Plato 1953:249–288). According to Michael Jackson, however, some of the best examples of the limits of rational thought may be found at the beginning of the Sung dynasty in China (ca. 960 BCE). As one Zen master put it, "We have not to overcome contradiction but to live it" (Jackson 2007:xxii).

Chapter 1

1. Some ethnographies of China have begun to put an emphasis on individual people and sentiments (Liu 2000; Yan 2003; Fong 2004; Kleinman et al. 2011), and some scholars argue that individualization of Chinese society is taking place (Yan 2009; Hansen and Svarverud 2010).

2. "Guomindang" is the Mandarin term for the Nationalist Party using pinyin romanization. The Nationalist Party was founded by Sun Yatsen in 1912.

Chapter 2

1. Devereux (1953), Fortes (1969), and others have looked at the ambivalence of parent-child relations from the perspective of the parents as well as the children. As Milner presents it, the psychosocial development of the individual is seen as being bound up with a three-generation cycle. It begins with the complete dependence of the infant on

its mother, moves on to childhood when the father (in some cases) comes significantly into the picture, then proceeds through adolescence, with its undercurrents of intergenerational tensions associated with the strains of sexual and moral maturation. Next come marriage and then parenthood, which often bring new stresses in their wake, and finally the completion of the cycle when the initial generations become grandparents and revert to dependence in their old age (Milner 1938, cited in Fortes 1969:219).

2. Here I am drawing on Teresa Kuan's reading of the book *Spring City Evening News*. The popular parenting expert and journalist Lu Xun, who goes by the name of Intimate Sister (Zhixin Jiejie), published the interview in a chapter of her book titled *The Call for Education for Quality*. Lu has established a periodical for children and their parents, tours the country giving talks, runs a hotline, and writes books for a popular audience (Kuan 2008:117). Her book *Tell Your Child, You're the Best!* was a top ten best seller in 2004.

3. The care and control (*guan*) of parents and the state converge in the general attitude toward romantic relationships between young people before marriage. Parents and school authorities, like the state, discourage romantic relationships between students. In 2002 a female student was excluded from a university in southwest China because she became pregnant (Milwertz 2003:11). During my fieldwork I heard rumors of similar cases at other Chinese universities. In 2005 the marriage law was revised, making it possible for students to legally continue studying after marriage and parenthood, but not many students took advantage of this change in the law.

4. Yu Hua, "When Filial Piety Is the Law," *New York Times*, July 9, 2013.

Chapter 3

1. I refer to the notions of the state and the government synonymously, as did the students I interviewed. Usually the term *zhengfu* ("government") was used by students. This term is different from references made to the "country" (*guojia*) or "motherland" (*zuguo*).

2. Cecilia Milwertz coined the phrase "control as care" to indicate Chinese women's acceptance of the one-child policy (Milwertz 1997).

3. Yan argues that the restructuring of society, beginning with land reform, whereby young people worked alongside their parents and earned their own independent work points, played a large role in the formation of a "youth culture" (Yan 1999:84, 86). After decollectivization, every man who was eighteen or older was allocated an equal share of land: in other words, village youths who were eighteen or older all received a share of land equal to that of the older villagers, and this was not affected by one's marital status. Furthermore, in the early 1980s the party-state began to loosen its earlier ban on rural-urban migration, and by 1993 the number of rural migrants to the cities had exceeded 100 million (Yan 1999:89). As a result, urban employment has opened a new world for young villagers, and they have experienced new lifestyles that older villagers have never heard of.

4. *Shige* is a compound character made up of the characters *lao shi* ("teacher") and *ge ge* ("older brother"), and in the same way, *shidi* is a composite of *laoshi* and *didi* ("younger brother"), *shijie* of *laoshi* and *jie jie* ("older sister"), *shimei* of *laoshi* and *meimei* ("younger sister").

5. Andrew Kipnis argues that the term "teacher" has become a common way of addressing strangers, especially when asking for assistance from people on the street or in a store. During the 1980s the term "master" (*shifu*) had replaced "comrade" (*tongzhi*) for this purpose. But during the first years of the twenty-first century, the connotations of "master" as a person without formal educational credentials have become a liability. "Teacher" implies not only that the person one is addressing is a kindhearted superior who is obliged to help (as does the term "master"), but also that this person has graduated from a tertiary institution (Kipnis 2009:217).

6. In fact, while Jia Ling was in England she was feeling guilty about neglecting care for her mother, who had recently been divorced from her father. Jia Ling's mother went through a long-term depression, and Jia Ling continues to feel guilty about being far away from her. However, she is the one who is now able to support their family financially, since her sisters' salaries are much lower by comparison and they each have a child to take care of.

7. Family metaphors also apply in relation to the difference between state-owned companies and private companies. Domestic companies claim, "We can only be the *concubines* of the state-owned enterprises or the *mistresses* of the multinationals" (Zhang and Ong 2008:7, emphasis added). In describing private companies as "concubines" and "mistresses," the idea is that these companies hold a secondary position in relation to state-owned companies, which have a place within the heart of political power, as they belong to the legitimate family of the state.

8. Actually, the understanding of the event is much more complex than it is usually made to seem in the Western media, which has tended to focus mostly on the students' desire for democracy and less on the frustration fueled by a scarcity of well-paid jobs (cf. Cherrington 1991).

Chapter 4

A version of this chapter was previously published as "Between Party, Parents, and Peers: The Quandaries of Chinese Party Members in Beijing," in "Governing Difference: Inequality, Inequity, and Identity," ed. Ravinder Kaur and Ayo Wahlberg, special issue, *Third World Quarterly* 33, no. 4 (2012): 721–735, www.tandfonline.com.

1. His idea was essentially that by making the hole in the toothpaste tube larger, toothpaste companies would be able to sell more toothpaste.

2. Kipnis argues that while a neoliberal approach masks hidden differences by "blaming the victim," *suzhi* discourse instead reifies differences (Kipnis 2007:389). He sees "blame the victim" discourses as a critique of the neoliberal welfare policies articulated in the rhetoric of Ronald Reagan. This style of discourse works by denying that, for instance, "welfare moms" are victims at all. It denies the relevance of structural factors to the explanation of their disadvantages and argues that if welfare moms cannot get off of welfare, they are just not trying hard enough.

3. *Asia Africa Intelligence Wire*, "College Student Killer Executed in Southwest China," June 17, 2004.

4. Anagnost writes: "Here, rather than the laboring body of the rural migrant, it is the labor of the child caught up in the culling process of school admissions and test scores and the labor of the parents to provide the child with resources to be successful in these endeavors that have become emblematic of the production of value in contemporary China. It seemed that what I was watching was nothing less than a substitution of bodies in which the extraction of value from one body was being accumulated in the other" (Anagnost 2004:191).

5. Bai Gang did not experience any pressure from his parents, as he had already far exceeded their expectations, and they had little understanding of the kind of life he was living in Beijing. Being a man, he did not experience any pressure to get married or have a child. Furthermore, as he had two siblings, he was not the only person in the family who could continue the family line. Like Sun Li, he had in a sense already taken part in a class journey, but unlike Sun Li, who had obtained a scholarship to study in the United States, Bai Gang was still in a liminal state, hoping to be able, through higher education, to transform his rural status to an urban status by obtaining a job that could provide him with a Beijing *hukou*.

6. Bai Gang said that generally his relationships with many of his old friends who had graduated had become tense, since many of them now had good positions and he found himself envious because he lacked these vital connections. He told me about a fight between two men on campus, a fight that was sparked by the jealousy of one over the fact that the other had "stolen his girlfriend." According to Bai Gang, the girl had chosen the man with the best *tiaojian*, meaning material conditions as well as personal connections.

Chapter 5

1. According to a brochure that was on display at the entrance of Color Baby, the Montessori motto of the program is "Children teach themselves."

2. The experience of taking my son to Color Baby is a clear example of the idea of participant observation being an oxymoron. It is impossible fully to participate and observe at the same time. This contrast corresponds to Hannah Arendt's contrast between *vita activa* and *vita contemplativa* (Jackson 2007:25).

3. However, concern about spoiling children in China did not originate with the single-child family (Tobin, Wu, and Davidson 1998:90). Long before the 1949 revolution, texts on raising children warned of the dangers of *ni-ai*, or "drowning a child with love." This concern has increased with the widespread tendency of viewing parents and grandparents as overindulging an only child. The Child Development Center of China, established with UNICEF funds in 1981, has a mandate to raise the quality of Chinese parenting and preschool education by coaching teachers and parents in nutrition, education, and "how not to spoil their children," teaching them that discipline is vital (Tobin, Wu, and Davidson 1998:93).

4. Liu's mother begins by forcing herself to eat specific kinds of food even when they make her sick in order to give her fetus the best nutrition. After Liu is born, she is fed at regular intervals. During her first year her mother starts training her memory with con-

stant questioning, and when she is eighteen months old her mother sets her to memorize Tang Dynasty poems. (Kipnis 2006:309).

5. Dewey was also the first modern Western theorist to visit and lecture in China. He gave more than two hundred lectures during his two-year visit to China. His speeches were translated into Chinese and published in journals and books. These books were reprinted ten times in runs of ten thousand copies, which sold out almost immediately (Qi 2008:257).

6. Before the May Fourth Movement, the Chinese language consisted of two forms: *wen yan* and *bai hua*. The former, *wen yan*, is a classical language; the latter, *bai hua*, is a vernacular language. Written Chinese, *wen yan*, was completely different from spoken Chinese in grammatical structure and vocabulary. I was also detached from real life, but reflected the symbolic power or language of the elite. Therefore the new intellectuals considered it to be an obstruction that restricted intellectuals' thinking abilities due to its complicated sentence structure, ancient vocabulary, and difficult orthography. It was regarded as a "half-dead" and "non-scientific" language (Qi 2008:265). This language reform meant that writers could use colloquial language and a subjectivist viewpoint that was very different from the Confucian moralizing discourse (Qi 2009:267). This language reform also had a great impact on the educational system. In 1921 the Ministry of Education abolished the use of *wen yan wen* at schools, and the vernacular language, *bai hua*, became a national language in both written and spoken forms.

7. It is worth noting that the rise of leisure culture in urban China has been actively promoted by national policies introducing leisure time (the two-day weekend in 1995, the week-long May 1 holiday in 2000), as well as local campaigns teaching municipal citizens how to spend their leisure time (Jing Wang 2001:64, cited in Kuan 2008:64). The public exercise machines that have been erected in many parks in Chinese cities also stand out in this respect. Jing Wang argues that the ideological and economic component to this development is that leisure culture supports the expansion of service industries. At the same time, he points out that from the public's point of view, leisure culture appears to be a sign of China's long-awaited progress toward Western ideals in its creation of an egalitarian public sphere and democratic consumption (Jing Wang 2001:64, cited in Kuan 2008:64).

8. His comment reminded me of Susan Greenhalgh's description of some of the birth planning cadres during the initial stages of the implementation of the one-child policy, who were designated "model workers," sacrificing their own families for the sake of the nation (Greenhalgh 2005). It seems that the model citizens of today embody the greatness of the nation through their *individual* talents rather than through sacrifice for the common good. Breinegaard has described a similar phenomenon in Japan, where Japanese students who have studied abroad and return to Japan are accorded special status (Breinegaard 2003).

9. The famous Chinese writer Lu Xun was part of the May Fourth Movement, and he was among the first Chinese writers to use colloquial Chinese in their work.

10. Rachel Murphy describes the dilemma of village schoolteachers, who are often not secure in their employment and are evaluated by their performance on professional exams and in teaching competitions, as well as by the grades of their students (Murphy 2004:12).

As a result, many teachers respond by outwardly pursuing *suzhi jiaoyu* while covertly prioritizing exams. One teacher expressed it like this: "We have to deal with the demands of both exams and *suzhi* education, and they are not compatible because extra-curricular activities take time away from study. So we have 'interest hobby groups' on Wednesday afternoons, but we use this time to coach the students" (Murphy 2004:13).

11. Epigraph to Michael Jackson's *In Sierra Leone* (2004).

12. I am paraphrasing Marx's elaboration on a comment of Hegel's in *The Eighteenth Brumaire of Louis Bonaparte* (1934).

Chapter 6

Material from this chapter previously appeared in Susanne Bregnbæk (2011), "A Public Secret: 'Education for Quality' and Suicide among Chinese Elite University Students," *Learning and Teaching* 4, no. 3:18–36.

1. When I visited the psychological counseling center at Beijing University, I experienced the same reluctance to talk about the number of cases at Beijing University. The psychologist to whom I spoke saw broken love relationships as one of the main reasons driving people to commit suicide.

2. Here I would like to point out that it is in no way my intention to blame the universities for these cases of suicide.

3. According to Bunkenborg, the connection between sudden death and subhealth was established when two cases of sudden death at Tsinghua University, that of a thirty-six-year-old lecturer, Jiao Lianwei, and that of a forty-six-year-old professor, Gao Wenhuan, were reported by the media as resulting from over-exhaustion (Bunkenborg 2009:199).

4. The Chinese educational system has many similarities with the Japanese educational system, which is also (in)famous for exerting strong pressure on Japanese children, leading to high suicide rates. The educational system has been subject to criticism for valuing conformity rather than creativity and rote memory rather than individual thinking, and demands for reform have increased over the past decade. Despite harsh criticism, however, there have been few changes (Breinegaard 2005:76). According to Anne Allison, the road to success in Japanese schools depends on "a willingness to bend to the authority of the school system and an ability to mimetically reproduce its structure of endless surveillance, constant exams, and habitual memorization" (Allison 1996:xiv, cited in Fong 2006:116). Just as the Japanese educational system is focused on the production of "sameness," so too in China people similarly refer to the notion of following "the trend," a trend of eschewing play and other pastimes, studying diligently in order to pass exams, and achieving high status, most often meaning having a high salary.

5. Jerome Bruner defines "subjunctivity" as "to be trafficking in human possibilities" (S. R. Whyte 1997:24).

6. Cited with permission from the author.

7. Wu Fei's work is a contribution to a trend of wishing to sinicize social theory of which I am somewhat skeptical, as I rather see the aim of anthropology as being able to look at the intersection between the universal and the particular. Sinicizing anthropology

to me seems to be a form of identity politics disguised as social theory, and I think keeping the two apart has the greater potential for mutual understanding.

8. Emile Durkheim's famous book *Suicide* (1899) was groundbreaking in its argument that suicide, possibly the most individualistic act, is to be understood as a social act. Durkheim argued that suicide is telling of how the individual relates to society. High rates of suicide therefore reflect the malaise of the social body. According to Durkheim, there are three aetiological types of suicide: egoistic suicide, altruistic suicide, and anomic suicide (the fourth type, the fatalistic suicide, is merely mentioned in a footnote as a theoretical category—the opposite of anomic suicide).

9. See, for example, Hillman (1976), Menninger (1938), and Schneidman (1974).

10. According to Wu Fei, "loss of personhood" refers to both loss of *lian* and loss of *mian*. Both concepts can be translated as "face" and can broadly be translated as "moral face" and "social face." The former thus refers to the image of a person and the latter to his or her ability to carry out his or her social role (Wu 2005:208–210).

11. I will leave aside the question of whether this focus on personhood and social status could be rephrased as linked to a question of agency, since an in-depth analysis of suicide falls outside the scope of this book.

12. According to Mary Douglas, taboo protects the consensus of how the world is organized (Douglas [1966] 2006:xi). It reduces uncertainty, since ambiguity is threatening the maintenance of the social order. Taboo confronts the ambiguous and is shunted aside, into the category of the sacred. In her writings on taboo, Mary Douglas refers to dirt and cleanliness and the symbolic categorization of the universe within a religious framework across societies. However, it seems to me that the Chinese state works in ways that can be understood in similar terms.

Conclusion

1. "Xi Jinping's Vision: Chasing the Chinese Dream," *The Economist*, May 4, 2013.

2. My friend Marie Høgh Thøgersen brought this motif to my attention.

References

Alber, Erdmute, Sjaak van der Geest, and Susan Reynolds Whyte. 2008. *Generations in Africa: Connections and Conflicts*. Berlin: Münster Lit.

Anagnost, Ann. 2004. "The Corporeal Politics of Quality (*Suzhi*)." *Public Culture* 16(2): 189–208.

Arendt, Hannah. (1958) 1998. *The Human Condition*. Chicago: University of Chicago Press.

———. 1963. "Eichmann in Jerusalem." *New Yorker*, February 16.

Ariès, Philippe. (1960) 1996. *Centuries of Childhood*. London: Random House.

Aristotle. (1946) 1997. Politik. Translated into Danish by W. Norvin and P. Fuglsang. Copenhagen: Gyldendal.

Asia Africa Intelligence Wire. 2004. "College Student Killer Executed in Southwest China." June 17.

Bai, Limin. 2005. *Shaping the Ideal Child: Children and Their Primers in Late Imperial China*. Hong Kong: Chinese University Press.

Baker, Hugh D. R., and Stephan Feuchtwang, eds. 1991. *An Old State in New Settings: Studies in the Social Anthropology of China in Memory of Maurice Freedman*. Oxford: JASO.

Bateson, Gregory. (1972) 2000. *Steps to an Ecology of Mind*. Chicago: University of Chicago Press.

Benjamin, Walter. 1968. *Illuminations*. New York: Harcourt.

Biehl, João, Byron Good, and Arthur Kleinman, eds. 2007. *Subjectivity: Ethnographic Investigations*. Berkeley: University of California Press.

Bloch, Ernst. 1986. *The Principle of Hope*. Translated by Neville Plaice, Stephen Plaice, and Paul Knight. Cambridge, MA: MIT Press.

Bourdieu, Pierre. 1990. *The Logic of Practice*. Translated by Richard Nice. Stanford: Stanford University Press.

Brandtstädter, Susanne, and Goncalo D. Santos, eds. 2009. *Chinese Kinship: Contemporary Anthropological Perspectives*. New York: Routledge.

Bray, Francesca. 1997. "Reproductive Hierarchies." In *Technology and Gender: Fabrics of Power in Late Imperial China*, 335–368. Berkeley: University of California Press.

———. 2009. "Becoming a Mother in Late Imperial China: Maternal Doubles and the Ambiguity of Fertility." In *Chinese Kinship: Contemporary Anthropological Perspectives*, edited by Susanne Brandtstädter and Goncalo D. Santos, 179–181. London: Routledge.

Breinegaard, Janne. 2005. "Reworking Difference: An Analysis of Gender and Internationalist Discourses in Urban Contemporary Japan." Master's thesis, Institute of Anthropology, University of Copenhagen.

Brown, Norman O. (1959) 1989. *Life against Death: The Psychoanalytical Meaning of History*. Middletown, CT: Wesleyan University Press.

Bruner, Jerome. 1996. *The Culture of Education*. Cambridge, MA: Harvard University Press.

Bunkenborg, Mikkel. 2009. "Porous Persons and Empty Disorders: Producing Healthy People in Rural North China." Ph.D. diss., Institute of Anthropology, Copenhagen, University of Copenhagen.

Buruma, Ian. 2003. "Asiaworld: Om temaparker og den asiatiske verden som en dårlig kopi af den vestlige" ["Asiaworld: On theme-parks and the Asian world as a bad copy of the Western World"]. *Lettre* 2:17–21.

Cherrington, Ruth. 1991. *China's Students: The Struggle for Democracy*. London and New York: Routledge.

Chu, Godwin C., and Francis L. K. Hsu. 1983. *China's New Social Fabric*. London and Boston: Kegan Paul International.

Chua, Amy. 2011. *Battle Hymn of the Tiger Mother*. New York: Bloomsbury.

deMause, Lloyd, ed. 1974. *The History of Childhood*. New York: Psychohistory Press.

Desjarlais, Robert. 1997. *Shelter Blues: Sanity and Selfhood among the Homeless*. Philadelphia: University of Pennsylvania Press.

Deutsch, Francine. 2004. "How Parents Influence the Life Plans of Graduating Chinese University Students." *Journal of Comparative Family Studies* 35(3): 393–421.

Devereux, George. 1953. "Why Oedipus Killed Laius: A Note on the Complementary Oedipus Complex in Greek Drama." *International Journal of Psycho-Analysis* 34:132–141.

———. 1967. *From Anxiety to Method in the Behavioral Sciences*. The Hague: Mouton.

Dewey, John. 1964. *On Education: Selected Writings*. Chicago: University of Chicago Press.

Dikötter, Frank. 1998. *Imperfect Conceptions: Medical Knowledge, Birth Defects, and Eugenics in China*. New York: Columbia University Press.

Douglas, Mary. (1966) 2006. *Purity and Danger*. London: Routledge.

Durkheim, Émile. (1952) 2006. *Suicide*. London: Routledge Classics.

The Economist. "Xi Jinping's Vision: Chasing the Chinese Dream." May 4, 2013.

Erikson, Erik H. (1968) 1994. *Identity, Youth, and Crisis*. New York: W. W. Norton.

Evans, Harriett. 2008. *The Subject of Gender: Daughters and Mothers in Urban China*. New York: Rowman and Littlefield.

Farquhar, Judith. 2002. *Appetites: Food and Sex in Post-Socialist China*. Durham, NC: Duke University Press.

Ferguson, James. 2013. "Declarations of Dependence: Labour, Personhood, and Welfare in Southern Africa." *Journal of the Royal Anthropological Institute* (N.S.) 19:223–242.

Feuchtwang, Stephen. 2002. "Remnants of Revolution in China." In *Postsocialism: Ideals, Ideologies, and Practices in Eurasia*, edited by C. M. Hann, 196–215. London: Routledge.

Fong, Vanessa. 2004. *Only Hope: Coming of Age under China's One-Child Policy*. Stanford: Stanford University Press.

————. 2011. *Paradise Redefined: Transnational Chinese Students and the Quest for Flexible Citizenship in the Developed World*. Stanford: Stanford University Press.

Fortes, Meyer. 1949. *The Web of Kinship among the Tallensi*. London: Oxford University Press.

————. (1959) 1981. *Oedipus and Job in West African Religion*. New York: Octagon.

Fortes, M., and E. E. Evans-Pritchard, eds. 1987. *African Political Systems*. New York: KPI Ltd. in association with the International African Institute.

Fortes, Meyer, and J. Goody. 1987. *Religion, Morality, and the Person: Essays on Tallensi Religion*. Cambridge and New York: Cambridge University Press.

Foucault, Michel. 1977. *Discipline and Punish: The Birth of the Prison*. New York: Pantheon Books.

Freedman, Maurice. 1958. *Lineage Organization in Southeastern China*. London: University of London, Athlone Press.

————. 1979. *The Family in China, Past and Present: The Study of Chinese Society*. Stanford: Stanford University Press.

Freud, Sigmund. 1957. *Standard Edition of the Complete Psychological Work of Sigmund Freud*. Translated and edited by James Strachey. London: Hogarth Press.

Greenhalgh, Susan. 2003. "Planned Births, Unplanned Persons: 'Population' in the Making of Chinese Modernity." *American Ethnologist* 30(2): 196–215.

Greenhalgh, Susan, and Edwin A. Winckler. 2005. *Governing China's Population: From Leninist to Neoliberal Biopolitics*. Stanford: Stanford University Press.

Gullestad, Marianne. 2002. *Det norske sett med nye øyne*. Oslo: Universitetsforlaget.

Hage, Ghassan. 1996a. "The Spatial Imaginary of National Practices: Dwelling-Domesticating/Being-Exterminating." *Society and Space* 14 (Environment and Planning): 463–485.

————. 1996b. *White Nation: Fantasies of White Supremacy in a Multicultural Society*. Sydney: Pluto.

————. 2003. *Against Paranoid Nationalism: Searching for Hope in a Shrinking World*. London: Merlin.

Hansen, Mette Halskov. 2006. "In the Footsteps of the Communist Party: Dilemmas and Strategies." In *Doing Fieldwork in China*, edited by Maria Heimer and Stig Thøgersen, 81–95. Copenhagen: NIAS Press.

Hansen, Mette Halskov, and Rune Svarverud. 2010. *I-China: The Rise of the Individual in Modern Chinese Society*. Copenhagen: NIAS Press.

Heimer, Maria, and Stig Thøgersen, eds. 2006. *Doing Fieldwork in China*. Copenhagen: NIAS Press.

Hillman, James. 1976. *Suicide and the Soul*. Zurich: Spring Publications.

Hoffman, Lisa. 2001. "Guiding College Graduates to Work: Social Construction of Labor Markets in Dalian." In *China Urban: Ethnographies of Contemporary Culture*, edited by Nancy N. Chen et al., 43–66. Durham, NC: Duke University Press.

Howlett, Zachary. "China's Examination Fever and the Fabrication of Fairness: 'My Generation Was Raised on Poisoned Milk.'" Unpublished manuscript.

Hsu, Francis L. K. 1963. *Clan, Caste, and Club*. New York: Van Nostrand-Reinhold.

―――. 1967. *Under the Ancestors' Shadow: Kinship, Personality, and Social Mobility in China*. Stanford: Stanford University Press.

Huang, Quanyu. 2001. *Suzhi Jiaoyu zai Meiguo* (Education for Quality in the U.S.). Guangzhou: Guangdong Educational Press.

Hulbert, Ann. 2007. "Re-education." *New York Times*, April 1.

Hustvedt, Siri. 1998. *Yonder*. London: Henry Holt.

Ikels, Charlotte. 2004. *Filial Piety: Practice and Discourse in Contemporary East Asia*. Stanford: Stanford University Press.

Jackson, Michael. 1995. *At Home in the World*. Durham, NC: Duke University Press.

―――. 1996. *Things as They Are: New Directions in Phenomenological Anthropology*. Bloomington: Indiana University Press.

―――. 1998. *Minima Ethnographica: Intersubjectivity and the Anthropological Project*. Chicago: University of Chicago Press.

―――. 2004. *In Sierra Leone*. Durham, NC: Duke University Press.

―――. 2005. *Existential Anthropology: Events, Exigencies, and Effects*. New York: Berghahn Books.

―――. 2006. *The Accidental Anthropologist: A Memoir*. Dunedin: Longacre Press.

―――. 2006. *The Politics of Storytelling: Violence, Transgression, and Intersubjectivity*. Copenhagen: Museum Tusculanum Press.

―――. 2007. *Excursions*. Durham, NC: Duke University Press.

―――. 2009. *The Palm at the End of the Mind: Relatedness, Religiosity, and the Real*. Durham, NC: Duke University Press.

―――. 2011. *Life within Limits: Well-being in a World of Want*. Durham, NC: Duke University Press.

―――. 2013. *The Wherewithal of Life: Ethics, Migration, and the Question of Well-being*. Berkeley: University of California Press.

James, William. 1950. *The Principles of Psychology*. New York: Dover Publications.

Jing, Jun, ed. 2000. *Feeding China's Little Emperors: Food, Children, and Social Change*. Stanford, CA: Stanford University Press.

Kant, Immanuel. (1785) 1966. *The Moral Law*. Translated by H. J. Paton. London: Hutchinson University Library.

Kipnis, Andrew. 2006. "Suzhi: A Keyword Approach." *China Quarterly* 186 (June): 295–313.

―――. 2007. "Neoliberalism Reified: Suzhi Discourse and Tropes of Neoliberalism." *Journal of the Royal Anthropological Institute* (N.S.) 13:383–400.

―――. 2009. "Education and the Governing of Child-Centered Relatedness." In *Chinese Kinship: Contemporary Anthropological Perspectives, edited by Susanne* Brandtstädter and Goncalo D. Santos, 204–223. London: Routledge.

―――. 2011. *Governing Educational Desire: Culture, Politics, and Schooling in China*. Chicago: University of Chicago Press.

Kleinman, Arthur. 2006. *What Really Matters: Living a Moral Life Amidst Uncertainty and Danger*. Oxford and New York: Oxford University Press.

Kleinman, Arthur, and Joan Kleinman. 1996. "Suffering and Its Professional Transformation: Toward an Ethnography of Interpersonal Experience." In *Things as They Are: New Directions in Phenomenological Anthropology*, edited by Michael Jackson, 169–196. Bloomington: Indiana University Press:

Kleinman, Arthur, Yan Yunxiang, Jing Jun, Sing Lee, Everett Zhang, Pan Tianshu, Wu Fei, and Guo Jinhua, eds. 2011. *Deep China: The Moral Life of the Person. What Anthropology and Psychiatry Tell Us about China Today*. Berkeley: University of California Press.

Kuan, Teresa. 2008. "Adjusting the Bonds of Love: Parenting, Expertise, and Social Change in a Chinese City." Ph.D. diss., Faculty of the Graduate School of Anthropology, University of California.

———. 2011. "The Heart Says One Thing but the Hand Does Another: A Story about Emotion-Work, Ambivalence, and Popular Advice for Parents." *China Journal* 65 (January).

Laing, R. D. (1960) 1983. *The Divided Self: An Existential Study in Sanity and Madness*. Harmondsworth: Penguin Books.

Liu, Weihua, and Zhang Xinwu. 2000. *Hafo nuhai Liu Yiting* [Harvard Girl Liu Yiting]. Beijing: Zuojia Chubanshe.

Liu, Xin. 2000. *In One's Own Shadow: An Ethnographic Account of the Condition of Post-Reform Rural China*. Berkeley: University of California Press.

Lucht, Hans. 2012. *Darkness before Daybreak: African Migrants Living on the Margins in Southern Italy Today*. Berkeley: University of California Press.

Mannheim, Karl. (1927) 1952. *Essays on the Sociology of Knowledge*. London: Routledge.

Mauss, Marcel. (1925) 2006. *The Gift*. London: Routledge Classics.

Menninger, Karl. 1938. *Man against Himself*. New York: Harcourt.

Milwertz, Cecilia N. 1997. *Accepting Population Control: Urban Chinese Women and the One-Child Family Policy*. Richmond: Curzon.

———. 2003. "Activism against Domestic Violence in the People's Republic of China." *Violence against Women* 9(6): 630–655.

Mitchell, Steven A. 1995. *Hope and Dread in Psychoanalysis*. New York: Basic Books.

Mooney, Paul. 2005. "Campus Life Proves Difficult for China's Little Emperors." *Chronicle of Higher Education*, November 25.

Murphy, Rachel. 2004. "Turning Peasants into Modern Chinese Citizens: 'Population Quality' Discourse, Demographic Transition, and Primary Education." *China Quarterly* 177:1–20.

Ong, Aihwa. 2006. *Neoliberalism as Exception: Mutations in Citizenship and Sovereignty*. Durham, NC: Duke University Press.

Ortner, Sherry B. 2003. *New Jersey Dreaming: Capital, Culture, and the Class of '58*. Durham, NC: Duke University Press.

Pieke, Frank N. 2009) *The Good Communist: Elite Training and State Building in Today's China*. Cambridge: Cambridge University Press.

Plato. 1953. *Platons skrifter* [*Writings by Plato*]. Translated by C. Hoeg and H. Ræder, Copenhagen: Hans Reitzels Forlag.

Qi, Jie. 2008. "A History of the Present: Chinese Intellectuals, Confucianism, and Pragmatism." In *Inventing the Modern Self and John Dewey*, edited by T. S. Popkewitz. 255–279. New York: Palgrave Macmillan.

Rosen, Stanley. 1984. "New Directions in Secondary Education." In *Contemporary Chinese Education*, edited by R. Hayboe, 65–92. New York: M. E. Sharp.

———. 2004. "The State of Youth/Youth and the State in Early 21st Century China: The Triumph of the Urban Rich?" In *State and the Society in 21st-Century China: Crisis, Contention, and Legitimation*, edited by Peter Hays Gries and Stanley Rosen, chapter 8. London: Routledge.

Sangren, Steven P. 1987. *History and Magical Power in a Chinese Community*. Stanford: Stanford University Press.

———. 2013. "The Chinese Family as Instituted Fantasy: Or, Rescuing Kinship Imaginaries from the Symbolic." *Journal of the Royal Anthropological Institute* 19(2): 279–299.

Schneidman, Edwin. 1974. *The Deaths of Man*. Baltimore: Penguin Books.

Sen, Amartya. 1988. *The Standard of Living*. Edited by Geoffrey Hawthorn. Cambridge: Cambridge University Press.

Si, Lian. 2009. *China's Ant Tribe: Between Dreams and Reality*. Beijing: Beijing University Press.

Sigley, Gary. 2009. "Suzhi, the Body, and the Fortunes of Technoscientific Reasoning in Contemporary China." *Positions* 13(3): 537–566.

Stafford, Charles. 1995. *The Roads of Chinese Childhood: Learning and Identification in Angang*. Cambridge: Cambridge University Press.

———. 2000. *Separation and Reunion in Modern China*. Cambridg: Cambridge University Press.

———. 2003. *Living with Separation in China: Anthropological Accounts*. London: Routledge.

Thøgersen, Stig. 2002. *A County of Culture: Twentieth-Century China Seen from the Village Schools of Zouping, Shandong*. Ann Arbor: University of Michigan Press.

———. 2003. "Parasites or Civilizers: The Legitimacy of the Chinese Communist Party in Rural Areas." *China: An International Journal* 1(2): 200–223.

Tobin, Joseph K., David H. Y. Wu, and Dana H. Davidson. 1998. *Preschool in Three Cultures: Japan, China, and the United States*. New Haven, CT: Yale University Press.

Tu, Wei-Ming. 1985. "Selfhood and Otherness in Confucian Thought." In *Culture and Self: Asian and Western Perspectives*, edited by Anthony Marsella. New York: Tavistock Publications.

Vigh, Henrik. 2003. "Navigating Terrains of War: Youth and Soldiering in Guinea-Bissau." Ph.D. diss., Institute of Anthropology, Copenhagen, University of Copenhagen.

Wang, Jing. 2001. "The State Question in Chinese Popular Cultural Studies." *Inter-Asia Cultural Studies* 2(1): 35–52.

Weber, M., and T. Parsons. 1930. *The Protestant Ethic and the Spirit of Capitalism*. New York: Scribner.

Whyte, Martin King. 1997. "The Fate of Filial Obligations in China." *China Journal* 38 (July): 1–31.

Whyte, Susan Reynolds. 1997. *Questioning Misfortune: The Pragmatics of Uncertainty in Eastern Uganda*. Cambridge: Cambridge University Press.

Winnicott, D. W. (1964) 1991. *The Child, the Family, and the Outside World*. London: Penguin Books.

———. 1974. *Playing and Reality*. Harmondsworth: Penguin Books.

Woronov, Terry E. 2007. "Chinese Children, American Education: Globalizing Child Rearing in Contemporary China." In *Generations and Globalization: Youth, Age, and Family in the New World Economy*, edited by Jennifer Cole and Deborah Durham, 29–52. Bloomington: Indiana University Press.

———. 2009. "Governing China's Children: Governmentality and the 'Education for Quality.'" *Positions: East Asian Cultures Critique* 17(3): 568–589.

Wu, Fei. 2005. "Elegy for Luck: Suicide in a County of North China." Ph.D. diss., Harvard University.

Yan, Yunxiang. 1999. "Rural Youth and Youth Culture in North China." *Culture, Medicine, and Psychiatry* 23: 75–97.

———. 2003. *Private Life under Socialism: Love, Intimacy, and Family Change in a Chinese Village, 1949–1999*. Stanford: Stanford University Press.

———. 2009. *The Individualization of Chinese Society*. Oxford: Berg.

Yang, Maifair. 2004. "Longer Contemplation." In *New Reflections on Anthropological Studies of (Greater) China*, edited by X. Liu. Berkeley: Institute of East Asian Studies, University of California, Berkeley, and Center for China Studies.

Yongming, Zhou. 2008. "Privatizing Control: Internet Cafés in China." In *Privatizing China: Socialism from Afar*, edited by Li Zhang and Aihwa Ong, 214–229. Ithaca, NY: Cornell University Press.

Zhang, Li. 2001. *Strangers in the City: Reconfigurations of Space, Power, and Social Networks within China's Floating Population*. Stanford, CA: Stanford University Press.

Zhang, Li, and Aihwa Ong. 2008. *Privatizing China: Socialism from Afar*. Ithaca, NY: Cornell University Press.

Zito, Anita, and Tani E. Barlow. 1994. *Body, Subject, and Power in China*. Chicago: University of Chicago Press.

Index